STOP
CONTROLLING
ME!

WHAT TO DO WHEN SOMEONE YOU LOVE
HAS TOO MUCH POWER OVER YOU

RICHARD J. STENACK, PH.D.

New Harbinger Publications, Inc.

Publisher's Note

This publication is designed to provide accurate and authoritative information in regard to the subject matter covered. It is sold with the understanding that the publisher is not engaged in rendering psychological, financial, legal, or other professional services. If expert assistance or counseling is needed, the services of a competent professional should be sought.

Distributed in the U.S.A. by Publishers Group West; in Canada by Raincoast Books; in Great Britain by Airlift Book Company, Ltd.; in South Africa by Real Books, Ltd.; in Australia by Boobook; and in New Zealand by Tandem Press.

Copyright © 2001 by Richard J. Stenack
      New Harbinger Publications, Inc.
      5674 Shattuck Avenue
      Oakland, CA 94609

Cover design by Blue Design
Edited by Brady Kahn
Text design by Michele Waters

ISBN 1-57224-246-9 Paperback

All Rights Reserved

Printed in the United States of America

New Harbinger Publications' Web site address: www.newharbinger.com

03   02   01

10   9   8   7   6   5   4   3   2   1

First printing

This work was inspired by clients of mine who sought therapy to deal with their control issues. While seeking my help, they also helped shape my thinking in this difficult area. They provided ideas and insights that can come only from struggling with control problems on a daily basis. I dedicate this book to them.

Contents

Foreword

The information in this book is based on my twenty years as a therapist working with control issues in relationships. My clients have been people who, perhaps like you, were struggling in controlling relationships. As we worked on their issues, they provided many insights that have made their way into this book. The examples I give all derived from cases of individuals in my therapy practice.

As I grow in my understanding of control, I am ever amazed at how broad a subject it is and how deep the roots of the problem go. I will focus here primarily on marriage and committed relationships, but the truth is that control can be found in all kinds of relationships. Control issues also affect a broad range of people.

If you are in a controlling relationship, it's important to realize that there are many others like you. It's also important to realize that control is actually a *process* between people. It is not something that just happens. If you are dealing with a process, it can be altered. You are not helpless. You can do something about the problem.

I will first talk about what may have made you susceptible to a controlling relationship. I will describe how controlling relationships happen, the things people do to control one another, what it is like to live in a controlling relationship, and how to break free from control if that is what you decide must be done. Finally, I will describe ways to avoid getting into another controlling relationship—ways to break the cycle of control. In all of this, you must understand that there are going to be exceptions to everything written here. We are, after all, dealing with human beings and humans come in a vast variety of packages.

I have also tried to describe what it is like to live free from control and to be a part of a relationship that does not have control as part of its makeup. If control is a large part of your relationship, you may come to the conclusion that there is no alternative. That is simply not true. You can develop a relationship that is not based on control.

I have organized this material in the format that usually works best in actual therapy. It is a simple process: awareness, understanding, change, and then prevention. Too often the first two elements are forgotten or bypassed. I have found that not paying enough attention to the awareness and understanding phases of treatment sets the stage for relapse. Before trying to build a structure, there must be a solid foundation. The first two chapters are dedicated to developing awareness, the second two chapters focus on creating a full understanding, the next three chapters are all about change, and the final chapter is focused on the future and how to prevent falling back into control. You will also find exercises, usually at the end of each chapter. They are designed to personalize the concepts presented in the chapters helping you apply what you read directly to your own experience.

Introduction

Sometimes it is hard to know if you are in a controlling relationship. You may have problems in your relationship but may not have examined those problems in terms of control. The first issue to resolve is whether or not you are in a controlling relationship. What follows is a series of questions designed to help you decide for yourself. Answering the questions will also help you begin to locate behavioral problems in your relationship.

_____ Does your partner not trust you?

_____ Is your time away from your partner tightly controlled?

_____ Are you accused of doing things behind your partner's back, such as having affairs?

_____ Is your money tightly controlled?

_✓_ Are you held accountable for what you spend?

_M_ Does your partner put you down, either when you are alone or with others?

_✓_ Does your partner make you feel foolish?

_✓_ Is your partner disrespectful toward you?

_✓_ Does your partner try to avoid being with you?

_✓_ Does your partner do things with other friends and not with you?

_✓_ Has you partner stopped trying to do fun things with you?

_____ Do you no longer feel you are friends with your partner?

_____ Do you and your partner no longer play together?

_____ Do you no longer feel loved by your partner?

_✓_ Do you feel the romance has left your relationship?

_____ Does your partner no longer pay attention to you?

_____ Are you taken for granted?

_____ Are you ordered instead of asked?

_✓_ Does your partner speak to you in a disrespectful manner?

_____ Are you afraid of your partner?

_✓_ Does your partner expect you to think the same as him or her?

_✓_ If you disagree with your partner, is there an attempt to change your mind?

_✓_ Are your ideas discounted out of hand?

_____ Is your partner trying to change you into something you are not?

✓ Is your partner trying to cut you off from friends and relatives?

✓ Does your partner criticize people you are close to?

_____ Do you feel you are competing with your partner and always losing the competition?

✓ When you are happy, does your partner try to bring you down?

_____ Are your accomplishments discounted or otherwise put down?

_____ Do you feel that you are never free?

_____ Do you feel always accountable?

_____ Do you get "in trouble" with your partner?

_____ Do you feel your partner is actually your parent and you are a child with no rights?

✓ Has the intimacy left your relationship?

_____ Is your partner sexually demanding?

✓ Do you feel sexually put down?

_____ Does your partner want to "have sex" rather than "make love"?

_____ Are you sexually taken for granted?

_____ Do you sometimes think of your partner as a stranger?

✓ Does your partner intimidate you?

_____ Has your partner ever been violent toward you?

_____ Is your partner obnoxious when you are with your friends or relatives?

_____ Does your partner obstruct your parenting?

_____ Does your partner manipulate your children against you?

_____ Have your children ever tried to boss you using methods similar to those of your partner?

_____ Do you get angry at yourself for appeasing your partner?

_____ Does your partner have a repertoire of looks and expressions that can frighten you?

_____ Are there "expectations" that you feel you must fulfill . . . or else?

This list is not comprehensive—there are many more such questions that could be asked—but if you found yourself often answering "yes," you can be reasonably sure the nature of your relationship is one of control. The purpose of this book is to help you eliminate control as a factor in your relationship. It may be that the only way to do this is to end the relationship, or it may be that changing the relationship is actually possible. In either case, if ending the cycle of control is your goal, then this book should help.

CHAPTER ONE

How This Life Got Started

Why would you let someone else control you? At the heart of the problem is a sense of inadequacy, a lack of faith in your own okayness. If you must rely on someone else to tell you that you're okay, you're in trouble. You are giving that person too much power over your self-image. You're setting yourself up to be controlled.

Low self-esteem is also the basis for trying to control someone else. The controller's key characteristics are insecurity and fear of abandonment.

A deep feeling of inadequacy can develop in a number of ways. It usually begins in childhood and often within the home environment, but there are exceptions in both cases. It is built on a set of false beliefs and fueled by the need for acceptance.

To understand control, you must understand the process that creates this inner sense of inadequacy.

How Insecurity Develops

"Please don't tell me I hate my mother." That was the first statement a woman made as she was about to begin her therapeutic journey. It is not surprising. There was a time when people in therapy were encouraged to blame all their problems on their parents as though parents were fully responsible for everything they did and for all the choices they made. Perhaps the first step should be to let parents off the hook, at least to a degree. While it is important to understand the role your parents played in how you think and how you relate to the world, you also need to understand the limits of that role and where your own responsibility for your life begins.

You were not born as a blank slate, clean and empty and ready to be written upon. You came into the world with what you might call a birth kit. This kit included things like the beginnings of a definable personality, a level of intellectual potential, and a whole set of inclinations and predispositions. These may have included such traits as shyness or boldness, engagement or aloofness, aggressiveness or fearfulness, and a tendency toward such things as diabetes, athletic prowess, physical clumsiness, alcoholism, depression, anxiety, and so on.

However, you were not born with an innate lack of self-esteem. There was no natural inclination to question yourself, your abilities, and your worth. Some of us may approach life very tentatively and cautiously, but that is not necessarily a sign of self-doubt. It would not naturally occur to a child to question personal value. Children are born taking themselves totally for granted. It just does not occur to them to question themselves. Children are all born like the cartoon character, Popeye. They all begin with the simple concept of "I am what I am." The concept of self-doubt has to be introduced by someone else. Children have to be taught to question themselves.

Parents Are Not Perfect

Parents do not typically stand at the foot of their infant's crib and say, "Let's really screw this one up." At the same time, there is no parent or set of parents that has done a perfect job of raising their children. In fact, the idea of perfect parents is not healthy. Supermom will only intimidate her daughter and make her feel like a failure, no matter what she does. She will also make it impossible for her son to find a woman who can measure up to her sterling performance. Of course, the same goes for Superdad. How does a boy come to grips with having a dad who is never wrong and always wins at the basketball hoop? How does he accept his own okayness when he grows up watching what he perceives as his dad's greatness? And how does a woman find, in the real world, a man as good as the idealized dad who always called her his princess?

Through the course of raising children, mistakes are occasionally made, and they occasionally have long-lasting consequences. That's life. It is a disturbing truth that humans are imperfect, but a large part of the essence of serenity is learning to accept that inescapable fact. One of the most frustrating aspects of our culture is our futile pursuit of perfection. For a child, the difficult task is learning that parents are actually human beings.

As a small child, you probably assumed your parents were perfect and any problems were your fault. Why? You needed a sense of safety, which came from fully trusting your parents' abilities. Remember how little data you had to go on, and how dependent you were on your parents as you tried to make order out of chaos. Also, since everything learned in your first months of life came from them, it was only natural to believe that they knew everything. So you defined words like *man, husband,* and *father* by watching the giant male. He is who you used to define *normal male*. And, of course, you understood words like *woman, wife,* and *mother* by watching the giant female, resulting in a definition of *normal female*. This also means that if your mom and dad have problems, you could have incorporated those problems into your understanding of normal.

To further complicate the issue, your parents were once children looking up at their own sets of parents, trying to understand and define the word *normal*. But because they were not raised in the same household, they had different experiences, which means they may have made different assumptions about what is normal. This, in turn, could have lead to different ideas about their marital relationship and how to raise children. They could have begun marriage not understanding that they had different definitions of *normal* and suddenly have found themselves at odds with each other.

Boy Meets Girl

Suppose a boy is born into a home with very little demonstration of affection. He grows up without hugs and warmth. He defines a normal household as one that is quiet and reserved. Suppose a girl is born into a home where there is a great deal of emotion, where love is expressed openly and naturally, and where anger is expressed as openly and spontaneously as love. In her home, issues are sorted out at the time they happen, and then the emotionally spontaneous environment returns to being one filled with love. Suppose these two people reach adulthood, fall in love, and marry. It will probably not take long before they discover that they have some very basic differences. They will approach family life from very different places and they will either manage to work toward a mutual definition of a normal relationship or have problems.

When children come along, the couple may find that their parenting ideas, based on their experiences as children, are very different. This offers the perfect environment for marital and parenting conflicts, where both parents think they are doing the right, or normal, thing even though they disagree with each other. They may become invested in trying to change their partner, who is perceived as doing things wrong. The result: more conflict.

Imagine a child trying to figure out what is normal in this context. In all the potential contradictions and conflicting messages within the home environment, there is plenty of room for confusion and for making false assumptions.

Perhaps the amazing thing is that most of us come out of childhood as well as we do. But few of us reach adulthood with no scar tissue.

Insecurity and the Fear of Rejection

Let us now look at an adult who has stronger feelings of insecurity. An insecure person is, by far, most afraid of rejection. If insecurity is actually the belief that there is something wrong with yourself, or that you are inferior in some way, then being rejected will be interpreted as a confirmation of that inferiority. To avoid having inferiority validated by another, you will do whatever you can to avoid being rejected.

How do you avoid rejection? There are a number of possibilities, but the simplest way to avoid being rejected is by not showing another person anything that might be an excuse for rejection. That means, more than anything else, not showing how you feel about things—or even showing that you have feelings. In terms of threatening conditions, the least threatening, as far as rejection goes, is revealing what you know. You can have a fact wrong and not be a terrible person. Revealing what you believe makes you more vulnerable. What you believe is getting closer to home, but beliefs can be mistaken and they can be changed. But how you feel is getting to where you live. Feelings reveal who you are. If you are insecure about yourself, then how others respond to you can become too important. If, for example, you show love and your love is rejected, then you can be hurt right to the center of your identity.

The truth is that most of us have some fear of rejection, just as we have some fear of any kind of pain or painful experience. As long as we come into this world imperfect, we will have sensitive areas that we will protect. For example, a child might tell all of his classmates that he did not study for an upcoming test when, in fact, he did study. Why the lie? It's emotional insurance. He knows that if he gets a poor grade, it will be less embarrassing if his classmates think he didn't study.

Most people are cautious about showing their feelings. But if they have a serious sense of insecurity, the defenses they construct become far too important to them, and hiding what is inside becomes a far too critical part of their interactions with other people. They may even come to avoid truly important things, such as loving. If loving someone is giving of your whole self, then having love rejected is having your self rejected in the most complete way. And that is the most painful experience of all. But you can avoid it by never truly loving anyone. You can marry, and even have a pretty good marital relationship, without ever taking the risk of actually loving another person.

There is an inherent problem with loving another person. It is not possible to truly love another without trusting. And to trust means to become vulnerable. Perhaps that sounds backwards. It's easier to think of trust as something one person gives to another: "I know my partner will never cheat on me." But there is another way of looking at trust. It has more to do with believing a partner will not consciously do something that might hurt you; knowing that you can become vulnerable to your partner.

Another problem with loving another is that, before two people can fully love one another, they must first surrender themselves to each other. And this means being able to share weaknesses, fears, and, yes, inadequacies, with each other. Only when your partner knows your vulnerabilities, and you know you partner's vulnerabilities, can the two of you go about the business of protecting each other from the outside. After all, marriage is supposed to be about helping each other, not competing with each other. Imagine two people standing together, surrounded by all the terrible monsters in the world. If there are children, they are huddled among the legs of the parents where they will be safe. The most foolish thing these two people can do, as the monsters are about to attack, is to start fighting with each other. That is why cooperation, not competition, is what it is supposed to be all about.

It is a short jump from being insecure to being afraid to love. You need a great deal of confidence in your love, and in the one who wants to love you, to become vulnerable to that person. If your sense of insecurity is greater than the love for another, you may not be able to overcome the defenses you have built and allow that vulnerability to occur.

How Insecurity Affects Parenting

There are many adults who have serious feelings of insecurity who are still fully able to love their children. This is true for many reasons. One is that children begin life totally helpless and dependent on them. To an insecure person, an infant may be perceived as the only person on the planet who does not represent a threat. Unfortunately, there are also some adults who feel threatened by anyone who gets too close, and they may have trouble establishing a normal loving relationship even with their own children.

To give an example of how different circumstances and reactions can be, imagine this: One man may feel threatened by his children from the time they are born. The demands of feeding, burping, changing diapers, bathing, and caring for them—in other words, nurturing them—may be too much for him. He's afraid of not doing a good enough job, that he will be inadequate. And so he backs off from them from the very beginning. Another man may be very loving to his infant and toddler but, when the child begins to question and disobey him, he may suddenly feel threatened. At that point he may start shutting out his child, rather than admit he cannot maintain authority or deal with challenges. A third father may be very loving to his children until they reach adolescence, but when they begin to challenge his authority, he will respond by growing distant. He interprets their behavior as a personal attack, and shutting down is the only defense he knows.

These examples do not address the situation where two insecure parents have different ideas about how to raise children. Insecure adults in this case may bail out of parenting at any point, in an effort to avoid rejection from their parents.

How Insecurity Grows in Children

Children need unconditional love and approval from their parents, and seeds of insecurity can develop when they don't get it. Sometimes children are denied the nurturing relationship from one parent but receive it from the other. But there are also children who find themselves in homes where both parents are unable to provide the love and approval they need so much. Lack of love and approval becomes part of their definition of normal, part of their definition of a marital relationship, part of their definition of parenting, part of their definition of man and woman, and so on, to their attempts to define the nature of life itself. It also can affect how they define themselves. Somewhere it dawns on them, "If my own parents don't love me, there must be something really terrible about me. I must be a horrible person because the one thing I know about life is that those giants are perfect, they are always right."

Remember, there is a need in children to believe their parents have all the answers. It is in adolescence, when they are flexing their abstract-reasoning mental muscles, that they begin to challenge this assumption. But even then they would really prefer to be proven wrong. The perfect parent safety net makes life more comfortable.

Many parents misunderstand what is going on when their adolescent children challenge them. Children may act as though their parents know nothing, they may try to outsmart and manipulate their parents, they may try to convince themselves that they have all the answers, but if they start to win this challenge, they become less and less happy. They actually become more afraid. They will fight their parents with everything they have, but they are happiest when they lose the struggle. Why? Think of how frightening life would be if you really had nothing and no one else to count on but yourself. At a deep level teen-agers know they do not have all the answers, they know they are not yet autonomous, and cannot make it out there on their own. So, to feel secure and safe, they must lose the challenge to parents and authority.

But insecurity can develop even when a child is well-loved. There are children who are loved by both parents and hit junior high school, for example, and experience peer rejection so severe that they are shaken from their naive belief in their own okayness. It may be something they have no control over, somthing that has nothing to do with their inner being. There they are, busily trying to define normal, and something outside the immediate family starts them questioning their own normalness. And parents, by and large, have little or no influence over this. Parents have very few levers they can pull to change things that are happening outside the home.

In the most extreme cases, children may experience some kind of trauma, such as an assault, and come away feeling responsible for what happened. They think that there are logical and personal reasons for everything that happens to them, and it is not often that they blame others, especially adults. Trauma of this kind can lead to deep problems, but it does not require this level of trauma to initiate feelings of inadequacy.

Personality Types: Givers, Takers, and Refrigerators

When children feel rejection, they have several options for dealing with it. Sometimes they try to fight back by being extra nice, extra giving. The theory is, "If I only love them harder, if I only do better, if I only do this or that more, then I will surely get the love and approval I need." They believe the parents or other outsiders are perfect and that they are somehow not living up to expectations. So long as they believe the problem is within themselves, they will remain trapped in a spiral of trying to please. They will try harder and harder with no results. The harder they try without results, the more convinced they will become that there is something wrong with them. Gradually these people become what I call *Givers*.

Others accept their perceived inferiority as part of who they really are. These children may rebel and try to reject their parents, or peers, or whoever is not accepting of them. If they believe they cannot improve enough to meet outside expectations, they may simply give up the struggle. Then they realize that negative attention is better than no attention. They lose motivation, and gradually develop the attitude, "I will take whatever I can get." In other words, to cope with insecurity, they become *Takers*. Often "whatever they can get" shifts from emotional attention to material things. Insecure parents may offer a materialistic love bargain because it poses no threat to themselves. Instead of love, they offer material things, and children accept the deal. This may lead to a purely materialistic orientation.

Some children become aloof, try to shut down their emotionality, try to live without feelings or the need for feelings. But this strategy gradually becomes a two-way street. They learn to not feel things or need feelings from others, but they also learn to not give away feelings, or to understand that there is a basic human need to give things, especially love, to others. This strategy is like the building of a wall a mile high and a mile wide with no door to let someone in or to let yourself out. It is very safe behind such a wall. There is no chance of pain and no chance of rejection. However, it is also very lonely. These children become the saddest people of all because they do not even know what it is that they are missing, only that they are missing something. They become totally unaware of what they are withholding from others, only that there is something unfulfilling about their lives. Their lives are empty, but they do not understand the emptiness. They look normal on the outside, but there is a coldness on the inside. Gradually, these people become what I call the *Refrigerators*.

Some children who experience rejection at home still manage to turn out okay. Perhaps they visit friends and watch how their friends interact with their parents and siblings, and they see that their home environment is not the only kind possible. They learn that they do not have to take responsibility for their parents' lack of love and attention. They learn that they don't have to judge themselves by what others think of them. They only have to judge themselves by what they think of themselves, and that the main challenge in self-judgment is to be as accurate as possible. I call these people the *Okay* people.

These groups are not clear-cut. They are simply personality models designed to help understand how people act and why. Think of them as people exhibiting certain patterns of behavior. Givers tend to send things, from themselves to others. Takers try to get things from others. Refrigerators stop all exchange. Okays try to keep things in motion between themselves and others.

Imagine a scale that measures giving and taking. Altruism, total selflessness, is at one extreme and total self-centeredness at the other extreme. The more you are a Giver, the closer you are to the altruistic end of the scale. The more you are a Taker, the closer you are to the self-centered end of the scale. Refrigerators and Okays are closer to the middle of the scale, but whereas Refrigerators tend to be aloof, Okays tend to be intensely involved with give-and-take.

No one is purely reflected in a single category. There are elements of Giver, Taker, and so on in everyone, even very secure people. You could be a combination of Taker and Refrigerator. Most Givers sort of expect something in return for their gifts. There are Refrigerators who began as Givers and were hurt, either so often or so deeply, or both, that they closed up their hearts to avoid pain but have not entirely surrendered their Giver traits.

The Resilience of False Beliefs

This is a common statement I hear in therapy: "In my head, I know I'm an okay person, but somehow I just don't believe it." There is a difference between thinking with the brain (logic) and thinking with the heart (emotion). Somehow, mistaken beliefs get through to the heart and it is very difficult to extricate them. Yet you have the power to change; you are evolving all the time. You have access to new information that can lead to insight which, in turn, can lead to change. But change is usually not something that happens on its own. You have to take charge of your life and make change happen.

In general, new beliefs are relatively easy to change, but the longer you have held onto a false belief, the more difficult it will be to let it go. The younger the child who develops doubts about his or her self-worth, the more resilient those doubts will ultimately be. Eventually those doubts become very hard to reject.

When serious self-doubt begins in, say, adolescence, it may do less damage. Remember the father who felt threatened only after his children began rebelling against his authority? Well, there is a very good chance that his teen-age children will simply label him a jerk and go on their merry way.

When teens reach adulthood, they often move away from the home. They have a fresh chance to redefine themselves. If they meet with success, if they find respect, acceptance, love—they can regain the shaken self-assurance and get back to a positive way of defining themselves. However, if problems continue, if they have negative experiences, the self-doubt may harden. They can develop a stronger belief in their inadequacy and start to move in an unhealthy direction.

The truth is that people can have their belief in themselves shaken at any time in their lives. You can suddenly lose your job, you can discover your spouse is having an affair, someone very close to you can suddenly turn on you; any number of things can happen to shake your self-confidence and cause you to question your identity and your worth. There is a natural tendency to take personally things that happen. You can feel a sense of fate, as though things that happen were designed to upset you or to prove you do not deserve success. True, things often happen for reasons, but the reasons do not always pertain to you directly. There are times when what seems to be happening to you directly is actually a by-product of something else.

Often, you could take on a problem that does not really belong to you. If you freeze your mind and start brooding over events rather than thinking things through, you increase the danger of starting a more serious problem within yourself. You can easily reach the conclusion that there is something basically wrong with you. If you already feel inadequate, these things can feel like proof that you are an inadequate person.

Inadequacy as the Prerequisite to Control

Again, it is your feelings of inadequacy, based on false beliefs, that make you susceptible to control. Think about it. If you are in a controlling relationship, you are in the process of surrendering your integrity. Becoming controlled is the gradual loss of integrity because you have to be brought down to a low enough level to put up with the unacceptable behaviors of the controller. For this to happen, you must participate in the loss of your integrity. So you ask yourself the question, "When was the first time my integrity was violated?" It may have been mental, verbal, or physical abuse, it may just have been a totally inappropriate remark, it may have been any number of things, but the message was, "You are less than me, you are in my power." When that happened, what stopped you from running for the hills? What thoughts did you use to keep yourself in the relationship? How did you justify a decision to accept this kind of treatment, that kind of attitude? There has to be some sense of, "This is what I deserve."

Yes, there are exceptions. There are people who may not have a strong sense of inadequacy who are actively choosing to remain in controlling relationships. Some do so out of religious convictions. Some choose to stay in controlling relationships because of financial issues, because they believe that two-parent families are better for children regardless of the nature of the family environment, because of extended family issues, and so on. There are issues of value involved.

The point is that when people actively choose to remain in their relationships, they are not trapped. It is what we have come to call marriages of convenience. There are reasons for the choice. In this work, I do not necessarily advocate divorce. Although I've directed much of my focus toward the person who is trapped and longing to escape, this book is also meant for those who choose to remain. Understanding the process of control provides tools to help avoid participating in the process. For those of you who want to break out of controlling relationships, it is important to understand that the foundation of the trap is your own insecurity. For those who choose to remain in your relationships, it is important to fight all attempts to introduce self-doubt into your thinking, for self-doubt is the element that allows the belief of personal inadequacy to take hold.

If you feel inadequate, acceptance from another is like a refreshing splash of cool water. Outside validation is intoxicating. The fact that it is useless over the long haul, that only internal validation—knowing from the inside that you are really okay—will have a lasting effect, is irrelevant at the time. Getting acceptance is the true motivating factor driving you if you are convinced of your own inadequacy. And you are willing to go through a lot of pain to get that acceptance.

Exercise: Conducting Your Life Review, Part 1

In the first three chapters of this book, you are asked to do a major exercise called a life review exercise. The purpose of the life review is to take the more general information presented here and apply it directly to yourself. If done thoroughly, it can be a great help in developing awareness and understanding of your personal situation, how you got to where you are now, and how control takes shape in your life. This can be the foundation you use to regain personal control and either end the controlling relationship you are in, or try to modify it into something acceptable.

You will need a notebook and time. This will not be assembled in one sitting. In the first part of your life review, you will examine feelings of inadequacy and where they came from. This involves getting to know your parents and other people who influenced your early development and your self-perception. You should plan on using several pages for each person. Begin with your father. At the top of the first page write: "My father as a human being." If he is alive, you may want to visit him. The point is to look at him as just a man, not your father. Try to take your emotions out of the visit. Try to see who he really is. If he is not alive, you will have to rely on memory. This may be harder to do objectively, without emotion. The goal in either case is to try to understand the man behind the father role. Was he rigid? Critical? Understanding? Supportive? Then do the same with your mother. Try to picture her as a human being, not your parent. Write down everything you can about her and your relationship with her. Could you talk with her? Did she understand you? Look at the family unit and try to see it as a system and write down how it functioned. Was it close-knit? Fragmented? Look at yourself growing up. What kind of a kid were you? Were you popular? Shy? A loner? Rebellious? Look at others who influenced you (siblings, friends, teachers, other relatives). The goal is to gain some understanding of the forces that affected your development, that led you to the negative and mistaken conclusions you reached about yourself.

As the thoughts about each person begin to accumulate, you should see a pattern for each of them developing. You should be able to draw some conclusions about the people who influenced your early beliefs. Did you, for example, discover that your father was stern and aloof, even distant? What conclusions did you draw about yourself based on his behavior? Were they negative? Did they lead to feelings of inadequacy?

Most importantly, can you see that they were mistaken beliefs? Did you find that your mother never quite fully approved of you? Did that lead you to judge yourself using an impossible measuring stick? Was there an older sibling always in the spotlight, while you were on the sidelines? Did you have a very tough junior high school experience with classmates making fun of you? Did these experiences make you feel inadequate?

Hopefully, from this you will begin to see where false beliefs that you have about yourself may have originated. This is the first step toward banishing them. Remember, take your time with this. You may spend weeks adding insights. Actually, as you go on, it will get easier to think of things to write. Just take your time and do not push too hard. Trying to get it all too fast will lead to omissions; whatever you write down could be important. The next two parts of the life review are designed to further develop this understanding of how you got to where you are now. But this does not mean you have to complete this part before reading on. The three parts of the review are designed to be works-in-progress and to complement each other.

CHAPTER TWO

How Controlling Relationships Happen

Why would a person who already feels inadequate seek a controller? People with low self-esteem do not go around asking potential partners if they are controllers, but they do seem to seek them out. They may say they were attracted to a sense of strength or determination or decisiveness in the other person, but there is also an element of control present that attracts them.

When does insecurity lead to control? As long as people keep being born imperfect, they will have some areas of insecurity. They have to deal with faults and flaws. They can be open about them or they can deny them. They can become defensive, hide their perceived weaknesses from others, and set the stage for the development of unhealthy relationships, or they can share themselves and create the possibility of a truly honest relationship—one in which they are accepted for who they really are, rather than for a false image they create to hide their true selves. It's all about accepting imperfection. If you can do that, you can then appreciate yourself, warts and all. It is only when you cannot accept yourself that the severity of your feelings of inadequacy goes up and you start hiding things from others. This is when the foundation for a controlling relationship may develop.

Not everyone who is insecure ends up in a controlling relationship. Begin with a vast population of people who experience strong feelings of inadequacy. Those feelings can be overcome at any stage of development. People can, and very often do, realize how they lost confidence in themselves and go on to regain it. People find healthy, nurturing relationships and begin to heal. Some people develop more individual (rather than relationship) problems, problems such as anxiety or depression. At many different points and for many different reasons, people find ways of either adjusting to these feelings, or not adjusting to them and, possibly, developing some type of problem. But not all end in controlling relationships. While many people start out as candidates for becoming part of a controlling relationship, not everyone who starts actually ends in one.

The Marital Bond

A marriage is supposed to be a beginning point. The creation of a new existence, a new unit that exists in and of itself. The marriage bond is supposedly something sacred. It has little to do with ceremonies, dressing up, throwing things like bouquets and garters, taking pictures, feeding each other cake, drinking champagne, and dancing the night away. Marriage is a look that passes between two people, the reaching of an understanding. It is a bonding between two people. It is the same with divorce. Divorce has nothing to do with court appearances and lawyer fees. A marriage ends the moment the spiritual flame flickers out.

Unfortunately, the kind of marriage described, the spiritual bonding that happens between two people, is seldom reality. There are many people living together, carrying the same last name, owning a photo album with pictures of an event, and adding up anniversaries, who were never married truly. As discussed in chapter 1, children become adults through a process of development. This means that, wherever you go, you take all of yourself with you. You carry all of your baggage into a marriage. If some of that baggage includes insecurity, that will become part of the marital relationship. If you have created a set of defenses to protect you from hurt, they will become part of the way you will interact with your partner.

It is normal to have some caution and some protectiveness toward your feelings. No one likes to have their feelings hurt and most people are cautious about trusting. Yet to love requires trust. Somehow, one must get from the careful and defensive position normally taken when dealing with another person, to one of trusting and being trusted. That is what the courtship period is all about. Courtship is the gradual process of letting down your guard and forming a trust relationship with another. The first year or so of marriage can be very stressful as partners compare quirks and idiosyncrasies, and try to accommodate each other. Problems begin when the defenses are too strong and inflexible, and when the trust is too difficult to give. Without the surrender, without the sharing, without the giving of trust, it is difficult to love and even more difficult to truly bond.

Unfinished Business

You may also take unfinished business into a marriage. Many people who did not receive parental approval look for partners with the same traits as their rejecting parents and continue their childhood struggle within their marriages. It does not happen at a conscious level; you don't actually say, "This one is just like my father, if I can just win his approval, the part of me that is hurting and feeling rejected and inadequate will be healed." But, in essence, that is what often happens. Most often, it takes the form of an unexplainable attraction toward someone. That someone may do you wrong, may act like a jerk, insult you, do all sorts of things, but you just can't seem to shake the attraction.

A person who was denied parental approval is like a person with a hole in his or her heart. There is an ongoing longing to fill that hole. That is how parents can continue to control their adult children, by continuing to withhold approval. The trouble is, and this is a very hard lesson to learn, that hole can never be filled. Even if your parents have a spiritual rebirth, even if they put on sackcloth and crawl to you on their knees with apologies and beg for the chance to love you, once you reach adulthood, the hole in your heart cannot be filled. It was the need of the child that was denied, not the need of the adult. On the positive side, you can learn to live with this hole in your heart, just as an accident victim can learn to live with a missing limb. The mistake you can make is to try to find a substitute parent to fill that hole. That is how some insecure people end up seeking controllers.

If you are searching for someone like the parent who did not approve of you, you are searching for someone who withholds approval. If you find someone like that, you will have put yourself right back into the childhood struggle. Until you are able to give yourself the approval you need, you will never fully participate in an equal relationship, and will never truly heal.

The Process of Control—The Evil Dance

The controller in a relationship is the partner who withholds approval. Once again, not everyone who withholds approval is going to be a controller. It is important to take a closer look at what makes someone a controller.

Why would one person feel a need to control another? There may be a number of answers to that question, but only one truly makes sense: *fear*. There is a basic assumption made on the part of a controller in a controlling relationship. It goes something like this: "If you are free to interact with others, you will discover someone better than me and then you will dump me." Underlying that assumption lies another one: "I am really a terrible person and if you discover this about me, you will reject me."

As disturbing as this concept may be, it is none the less true. Controllers feel just as inadequate as those they control. The controlling relationship itself is a fear-based relationship, fueled by a mutually shared sense of inadequacy. The controlled person may be victimized by the controller, and the victimization may take many forms, but it cannot happen without the active participation of the controlled person in the relationship. The typical controlled person is not controlled at gunpoint, they are not typically chained to a bed or locked in cells with steel bars. Yes, there often is abuse of some form, and there very definitely is brainwashing of one form or another, but there is also a tacit acceptance of control. This does not mean that breaking free is easy to do. Once a person surrenders to a controller, it is very difficult to get away.

Just as people do not evolve in vacuums, one person's control over another does not happen in a vacuum. It is a gradual process that may or may not start at the outset of a relationship. It is a subtle dance two people enter into, and happens gradually. They are awkward at first—they are unaware of the inadequacy issues—they just feel a kind of kinship, that there is something inside that they share. They learn to open up and start talking about things. They begin to share their histories, including the things that happened which hurt them.

Then begins a critical time. For a healthy relationship to develop—that is, for any truly healthy relationship to develop, one that will endure and flourish over a long period of time—two people must maintain a balance, an equality. It is not healthy to form a lop-sided relationship, where one person takes a leadership position, or seems to be the stronger, or the smarter, or the decision-maker.

Of course, there is no such thing as a relationship where both parties are equally talented, knowledgeable, wise, and so on. In every relationship there are areas where you will have a better way of handling things than your partner. But it is almost always the case that your partner will also have talents that you lack. Perhaps you are better at managing a budget while your partner is better at organizing the social agenda. The idea is to find the areas of talent and maximize the effectiveness of the relationship as a whole, rather than compete or allow either of you to dominate.

Unbalanced Relationships

In an unbalanced relationship, the one who seems to be stronger usually begins to resent having to carry more than half the load. But, perhaps even more important, the person who feels weaker begins to resent the feelings of weakness or inability to lead. This is the foundation for the classic love-hate relationship. Each may love the other person but hate to either have to carry the ball or to never get to carry the ball.

Add to this process two people with serious feelings of inadequacy, or just one person who feels inadequate, and a number of very unhealthy interactions can develop. The most common is that the person in the weaker, or more dependent, position, begins to seek ways to gain power in the relationship. This is not done by taking on some of the responsibilities. Instead, the dependent person begins to find ways to both control the other person, and to create and increase self-doubt in the other, for it is usually the weaker of two partners who tries to become the controller.

Let us return to the Givers, Takers, Refrigerators, and Okay people. All are susceptible, to controlling relationships. Remember, if you have issues with control, it is not a good idea to try placing yourself solely in one category or another. You can label yourself using the category in which you fit best,

but you need to look at how other behavior patterns sometimes characterize you as well.

Maybe a better way to understand how these types fit
together, would be to show them in action. Think of them, for
example, in terms of love. Givers are invested in sending love
from themselves outward. Takers are invested in receiving
love from the outside toward themselves. Refrigerators try to
be self-contained, neither giving nor receiving love (they sort
of stock their own shelves). Okays try to keep love moving,
from themselves toward the outside and toward themselves
from the outside. As you will also see in the following examples, not everyone who fits one of these descriptions is insecure. Secure people may also exhibit some of the above traits.

Givers

Givers, within the context of controlling relationships, are people with a strong sense of inadequacy who have come to the
conclusion that if they just do enough for others, they will be
accepted and esteemed. They are convinced that they are
flawed in some major way but that the flaws can be hidden by
overwhelming others with gifts. There are also Givers who do
not feel inadequate or flawed and are simply Okay Givers.

It will probably not surprise you to discover that the majority of Givers are women. Givers also can be often found in the
helping professions. Doctors, nurses, social workers, psycholo-
gists, counselors, and school teachers usually do what they do
because they have a desire to work with others and help them.
That drive can become a problem if you are not careful. If you
have a strong sense of inadequacy, there is a great deal of validation in helping others. If you provide comfort, you experience gratitude. If you are an effective teamworker, you find
professional respect. However, all the outside validation, no
matter how good it feels at the time you receive it, will not
have lasting value unless you can internalize it.

If you receive all that validation at work but leave the
workplace still feeling inadequate, you may end up wanting to

take that drive to heal, make better, or just to please, into your personal life. You may find someone who could be really great if he or she only overcame this or that flaw, and you may pick that person to fall in love with. If you have a strong sense of inadequacy, you may pick someone who also feels inadequate, believing that your partner's sense of inadequacy will prevent him or her from rejecting you. This tendency to pick someone who needs help, who needs to be fixed, is sometimes referred to as the broken wing syndrome.

There are a lot of Givers out there, and the good news is that most of them are healthy people. A lot of people simply want a very giving kind of relationship. When two healthy Givers get together, they create intensity in their relationship. The central focus of the relationship is providing and receiving love and pleasure.

When Givers love, they go all the way. But, and this is hotly debated, there really is no such a thing as pure altruism. Even when you put the change in the Salvation Army bucket, you enjoy the warm feeling you generate inside. To be truly satisfied in a relationship, the Giver must have a partner with an equal capacity to give. That does not mean the Giver actively and consciously needs equal giving, but the Giver needs to feel as important to the partner as the partner is to him or her. The atmosphere of giving must be equally intense and coming from both directions.

Insecure Givers

For a Giver with a strong sense of inadequacy, an inner conviction that there is something seriously wrong inside, the motive to give to a partner is no longer just to interact at an intense level, it is also to receive affirmation of okayness. The act of giving is almost a challenge to the partner. Unlike the healthy Giver described above, the insecure Giver is measuring the amount of loving that is coming back from the partner.

This is how the insecure Givers keep score, how they measure their partners' beliefs that they are worthwhile people.

Unfortunately, this process comes with a built-in trap. Because the belief of inadequacy is totally internal, it actually has nothing to do with the other person. The other person did not create the insecurity and cannot eradicate it. Therefore, no matter how much the other person loves, or at what intensity the other person gives, the goal of healing will not occur. The insecure Giver will never feel satisfied, will never feel that the partner has given enough to stop the yearning for more.

The partner will find himself or herself in a contest that goes something like this: "How much do you love me? Well, prove it." This contest will just go on and on. So long as the insecure Giver continues to give and to measure personal okayness by what is offered back, there will never be fulfillment, and the lack of satisfaction will be expressed. Of course, these sentiments are seldom voiced directly, but the message will still get out to the partner.

I don't mean to sound hopeless here. Conversely, a healthy relationship can be a great context for someone with serious self-esteem problems to begin the process of healing. It is that same healthy atmosphere—the genuine acceptance of the person with no strings attached—that allows you to reevaluate your core beliefs of inadequacy and begin to change them. It is more like this, "My partner clearly and strongly believes that I have value. I have believed the nonaccepting people in my life and concluded that I have no value. Who is wrong, my partner or the nonaccepting people?" If the answer is that the nonaccepting people are wrong, you have the start of the reevaluation process that can lead to healing.

Measure for Measure

In other relationships besides a love relationship, Givers with low self-esteem will give with similar intensity and similar underlying motives. They will always want to pay for meals, offer to do the driving, give presents for no apparent reason, and volunteer for everything. But they are also measuring what is done in return. Not that they want anything specific from others; it is the gesture that matters. They can be devastated when forgotten but embarrassed when remembered. They're seeking validation all the time. By always doing for others, Givers are also trying to avoid rejection: "If I do all these things for you and accept nothing in return, you will think I am a great person and not reject me. If our relationship were based on an even amount of giving, you might look at me more objectively and recognize how inferior or flawed I am."

Some Givers hunger for compliments only to reject them when they are given. If you say, "I like that outfit," the answer will be, "What, this old thing?" Or if you say, "I like what you did with your hair," the answer is likely to be, "Don't even look at me, I'm having a bad hair day." Unfortunately, over time, this Giver gradually teaches those around him or her to never offer a compliment. A compliment, after all, is a gift, a present, and who wants to have their presents rejected time and time again?

In general, Givers need to be cared for, they need to be loved and reassured of their okayness by those who receive from them. This is especially true in a love relationship because it is so very personal and open. For a Giver to be happy in a relationship, the partner must be as intense as the Giver. Unfortunately, insecure Givers often form relationships with either Takers or Refrigerators. This happens because they are still seeking approval of their non-approving parent, and gravitate toward a similar person in a partner.

For the Giver, this often leads to frustration and the feeling of not being fulfilled. If that happens, the Giver can become resigned to an unfulfilled life; try to change the relationship, possibly with outside help; get out of the relationship; or start the process of creating a controlling relationship. There is often an assumption that Givers are always the controlled, that Takers and Refrigerators are always the controllers. This is not true. Givers are just as capable of controlling as any of the others. Even Okay people can become controllers.

Takers

Insecure Takers are people who have given up on themselves, who truly believe there is something terrible and horrible buried deep inside, and have reconciled themselves to that identity. Once this has been done, they take on the job of hiding what they think is on their inside—from others and, ultimately, from themselves. They become extremely defensive and will never admit to flaws, mistakes, or anything that can be seen as negative. They will do anything to avoid criticism. Over time, they may actually start to believe the defenses, the many masks they wear, and believe that they are guiltless and others are always responsible for the bad things that happen.

Takers are generally not looking for approval from others. Their tactic is the opposite from that of Givers. With Givers the whole relationship has balancing the scorecard as its goal. For Takers there is no concern for balance; the scorecard has only one entry, what the Taker can get.

Like Givers, there is a population of Takers out there who are not insecure. They are merely self-centered people who do not care about other people. The supreme Taker is the sociopath, someone who is not equipped with such standard features as a conscience, or a sense of guilt and responsibility toward others. They see others as objects to be used. Anyone can be a target for this kind of taker.

Fending Off Predators

When it comes to relationships, there are sharks in the water. There are predators out there, looking for the weak, the naive and, yes, the insecure. There are people willing to take advantage of you to get what they want. There are users, whether their objective is seduction and a single sexual encounter, or a lasting relationship consisting of abuse and control. It is important to be careful where you place your trust. Courtship is a process that allows you to get to know your potential partner. It is best done slowly and with wide open eyes. Predators have trouble maintaining their masks over time.

Predators trick the innocent mostly when their victims stop being honest and start lying to themselves. When you get to a point where you want to believe the predator so much that you begin to filter out the clues of what the predator is really like, then you are most vulnerable. This is especially true if you are an insecure person. If you are convinced there is something wrong inside you, then you may become willing to compromise with reality just to be loved. Staying honest with yourself is the key to avoiding entrapment by a predator. Even if a predator is able to maintain the mask until after marriage, the victim must still be honest. When you discover you are in a relationship with a predator, you must either act in self-defense or participate in the control process through self-deception.

Addiction Problems

Many people with addictive personalities, that is, a proneness toward addictive behavior patterns, are also Takers. Addictive people must maintain a denial system. For example, an alcoholic has a strong investment in maintaining the myth that he or she does not have a substance problem. This is a personal issue that does not necessarily involve the outside. People with addiction problems are not concerned with what others think; they are actually trying to use the denial system to convince themselves that there is no problem. The trouble may start in a serious relationship. In such a case, they may need to enlist their partner in backing up the denial system. To stay with the alcohol, they cannot have a partner who points out the amount of alcohol they consume.

Just to complicate matters, there are also a great many insecure Takers with addictive tendencies. They may be more invested in controlling a partner because they have more at risk. They have a double denial problem to deal with: denial of an addictive problem and denial of the perception of personal worthlessness. The worse their addiction becomes, the more convinced they will be that they are worthless. At heart, the denial system is a sham—addicted people are not really fooling themselves about having a substance problem; underneath all the subterfuge they know the truth.

Takers in Relationships

As with the other examples, Takers do not always enter controlling relationships. Some find healthy partners and develop, what is for them, satisfying relationships. Not surprisingly, they are often attracted to Givers. When Takers find Givers, they think they are embarking on an ideal journey through life. To them, the flow (of anything from love to money to material things) from Giver to Taker must seem like a very natural and mutually satisfying arrangement. That is because the Taker does not think of the Giver's underlying expectation of also being a receiver. So, if Takers do not learn to give in return, they will either lose their partner or have to begin the process of controlling.

Surprisingly, Takers often do well with other Takers. They form a sort of business relationship. As long as each can maintain their part of the bargain, they can manage quite well. Of course, there is not a lot of love in such a relationship. Part of the definition of love is giving, and that comes from the deep desire to see the one you love being as happy and fulfilled as possible. Takers are not very good at focusing outward, so they often come up short in the love area. When two Takers are involved, this is often not a problem because Takers are the ones who have become convinced they really are messed up and do not deserve love in the first place. They have spent many years squashing their need for love. Most of them have become quite content operating a relationship on a materialistic and physically satisfying level. Those Takers who do need love are usually demanding of it and unable to return it.

So two Takers can manage a relationship as long as they both feel they are getting equivalent value from each other. This can take several forms. For example, a man may want to be sexually satisfied and his partner may want to own nice things. These are two criteria with little overlap. As long as both are satisfied, and their sense of the relationship is that it is balanced, value for value, it can endure. However, as soon as one Taker feels that the other is not fulfilling the contract, trouble begins. That is because Takers in a relationship together are usually very careful that they are not providing more than their partners. The trouble usually takes the form of a power struggle. Each complains about what they are not getting and each thinks the relationship is unfair. Most often, the power struggle leads to either the end of the relationship or the start of a control struggle with one becoming the controller and the other becoming some sort of perceived victim.

Takers can also do well with Refrigerators. Their general lack of concern regarding the feelings of others almost complements the Refrigerator's investment in not feeling things at all. There is a sense of safety for the Refrigerator; the wall is not assaulted and there is no threat of rejection. The price for this is to appease the Taker by giving in ways other than by expressing feelings. Perhaps the Taker just cares about money or sex. As long as the Taker feels satisfied, this surface relationship has the appearance of a real relationship.

For the insecure Taker, needs often escalate in a relationship. Over time, this person is likely to become dissatisfied because physical and material things can never really satisfy the inner self. This is the trap of the insecure Taker, just as hoping that external validation will be enough is the trap of the insecure Giver. No matter how much this Taker receives, there will always be a sense of unfulfillment. So the Taker keeps expecting more of whatever is being offered. However, when the Taker's demands become more than the partner is willing or able to supply, the relationship starts to fall apart. At that point, the Taker may scramble to gain control.

Refrigerators

Refrigerator people have chosen to hide from life. It was not a clear-cut decision made one morning. It was a very gradual process built on rejection after rejection. The child who just doesn't measure up may begin to feel the impossibility of ever measuring up. It is the child who keeps struggling to win approval, but consistently finds that approval is accompanied with a negative: "Yes, Johnny, that was a fine drawing . . . but the tree limbs are too straight." What does Johnny hear? Does he focus on the "fine drawing" part or does he focus on whatever follows the "but"? For people like Johnny, life is filled with sentences that contain the word *but*. Unlike the Giver who keeps plugging along trying harder and harder to win the acceptance that will never come, the Refrigerator slowly gives up the struggle, slowly stops showing his drawings, so he doesn't have to hear the criticism.

In many ways, Refrigerators can be as sensitive as Givers, but they cannot handle the pain of rejection. Gradually, they pull back from others. Over time they stop showing that they care and they stop looking for the acceptance they need so badly. They do not feel safe with other people because they, of all groups, have the most trouble with trust.

For Refrigerators, the idea of being vulnerable is too much to bear. They become so convinced that others want to hurt them that they feel incapable of giving someone else even a chance to get close. Suppose the whole class laughed at Johnny's drawing. How would Johnny feel? Now suppose this was a consistent pattern. When would Johnny stop showing his drawings? When would he begin to shut himself down? When would he choose to hide from life as the least painful alternative?

Refrigerators slowly become very self-contained, but at some level they know they are unfulfilled. They feel unfulfilled because there is love inside them; but it is a love they dare not offer. Through years of having things, including love, rejected, a person learns how to avoid the pain of rejection. It is much safer to hold the love inside and never express it.

The Cooling Process

It does not necessarily have to be a prolonged process that leads to the refrigeration of the heart. You can be in a single relationship, especially an intense relationship where you were completely vulnerable to your partner, and suddenly be rejected. You may be hurt so badly that a decision is made to never let the same thing happen again. How is this accomplished? By never becoming vulnerable again. How can you never become vulnerable again? By never loving again. For a Refrigerator, there is also a need to be loved buried deep inside. But, again, to ask for love and be refused is unbearably painful. And so the wall is built, brick by brick, perceived rejection by perceived rejection.

When you focus too much on the idea of rejection, when you are looking at everything that happens in terms of whether or not you are being accepted or rejected, then anything that happens can take on personal meaning. This can easily happen to people with strong feelings of inadequacy. They look so hard at the actions and words of others that they develop the belief that everything that happens around them is really directed toward them.

The process of personalizing everything that happens can lead to a number of common problems. You can easily become far too self-centered and lose realistic perspective. You can give everyone around you the power to set your level of okayness. You can end up living a life of almost hysterical and desperate attempts to please everyone with whom you come in contact. You can live on the edge of desperation—while those around you have no idea of what is going on inside.

Aloofness vs. Inadequacy

As with the other examples, there are many Refrigerators who do not have a serious sense of inadequacy. A better way to describe them may be to say that they are aloof. Becoming aloof can be a good strategy to adopt when you feel you are under personal attack. It is like pulling up a temporary shelter rather than building a permanent wall. Such a strategy, however, is an action, or possibly a reaction, to something specific. It is not a way of life. There are relatively confident and self-assured people who simply have trouble opening up to others. There are also people who do not have strong emotions within them. This is not something to try to judge; it is not fair to say that having strong emotions is good and not having strong emotions is bad. It is simply a truth that some people are naturally less emotional than others, and do not necessarily have problems because of this.

Trouble can happen when one person with a high level of emotions believes that everyone feels at the same level of intensity and tries to get a low-intensity partner to feel at the higher level. This leads to frustration, which often comes out in conversations:

"Honey, what are you thinking right now?"

"Nothing, dear."

"How can that be? You must be thinking something."

"No, I'm just sitting here relaxing."

"Our problem is that we just can't talk. You never have anything to say."

What if the Refrigerator in this example has simply learned the secret of meditation? The truth is that many people are very placid; they can go through life unruffled. They are like rowboats on a quiet lake. Many others feel the heights and depths of emotion. They are more like roller coasters. When two emotional opposites come together, they need to truly understand their differences to create a successful and fulfilling relationship. Many such couples form a relationship in which they learn from each other, and gradually each moves toward the other and they meet somewhere in the middle. The laid-back person learns excitement from the partner and the emotional person learns serenity from the laid-back partner. Givers, for example, are often the most emotionally intense. They may misunderstand their partner and struggle to help him or her to become more intense. The Giver could become frustrated that the partner "just doesn't get it" and end up becoming a controller.

Like Takers, Refrigerators can do relatively well with Givers, Takers, other Refrigerators, and Okay people. However, too often, the needs of the partner, any partner, eventually become so threatening to the Refrigerator, invested in giving nothing away, that absolute emotional exhaustion sets in. The relationship will either fall apart or the Refrigerator will begin the process of either controlling or being controlled.

Okay People

People who are relatively well-adjusted can also become caught up in controlling relationships. No one is immune. Suppose someone who has an average amount of confidence and a fairly good self-image meets a person with a very poor self-image and a strong sense of inadequacy. This can sometimes provide opportunity for the self-doubting person to heal and achieve a sense of okayness. But what happens if the person feeling inadequate does not respond positively to love? The insecure person thinks, "Others have told me I am worthless, my partner tells me I am valuable, who is wrong?" If the brainwashing has gone deep enough, has lasted long enough, was started early enough, the answer may be, "My partner is wrong. My partner just doesn't see my faults yet." This thought will quickly be followed by another thought: "And I have to make sure my partner never does see my faults."

Once again, the dance will begin. The inadequate person may become very critical of the Okay person. The goal will be to plant seeds of self-doubt: "If I bring my partner down to my level, my partner will feel no more adequate than me and will never leave me." In this version of the dance, the inadequate person, if successful, will evolve into the controller. In another version of the dance, the inadequate person becomes helpless and dependent on the Okay person: "I cannot survive without you, so you have to take care of me." This strategy is especially effective if the inadequate person adds an element of jealousy: "I know I am a burden to you and you might look for someone stronger. I must know where you are at all times because I am so afraid of losing you."

In this area, there is a pretty good rule of thumb: One way to measure a person's level of inadequacy is to measure that person's level of jealousy. It is true that there are many ways of dealing with feelings of inadequacy, but the primary one is expressing jealousy. Jealousy, after all, is nothing more than control wearing the mask of love. The truth is that jealousy has absolutely nothing to do with love. Jealousy is a form of possessiveness, and possessiveness is not a part of love. Jealousy is an under-the-table admission of worthlessness.

There are variations on the control dance, depending on how the inadequate person has adapted over the years. But fundamentally the Okay person either chooses to accept or reject the invitation to dance. If self-doubt is introduced into the mind of the Okay person, the odds of him or her engaging in the process increase. If the Okay person can spot and accurately understand the long-term nature of the dance, avoid self-doubt, and maintain a personal sense of being adequate, the odds of rejecting the process increase.

Okays can do well with Givers. They can provide a loving and accepting world. When Okay people are together with Givers who do not feel inadequate, each of them can learn the loving intensity level of the other, and they can grow together in love. Okay people can help Givers who feel inadequate; they can offer the very environment needed to challenge past assumptions of okayness. Okay people have more trouble with Takers and Refrigerators. The flow of love is not likely to move freely in both directions and this can lead to frustration in the Okay person. The result may not be surprising; the Okay person may leave the relationship or try to reshape the partner in a controlling relationship.

Choosing to Change

There is another point to be made about these categories. They do not have to be static. You are not doomed to live inside a label all your life; you can choose to change. A Giver with strong feelings of inadequacy may try to gain self-approval and change. A Taker may discover the emptiness of only taking from others and try to gain the joy of giving. A Refrigerator may want to learn how to open the freezer door and gain the warmth of love. Even some Okay people may need to develop more personal approval to feel fulfilled.

Most people do not change from their basic nature. This is not because change is such a major undertaking but because most people are so busy protecting their images that they are totally unaware of the possibility for change. Awareness has to precede change. The thing to remember is that habits, any habits, can be broken. To change, once a person knows that change is possible, takes commitment and a lot of practice. But, although it is relatively rare, it can happen. It is even possible for different people to help each other on their journeys of change.

For anyone who discovers they are participating in a controlling relationship, your awareness is the first step in ending or altering it. You discover that the nature of your relationship has been a dance and that you have both become so good you have reached the level of competitive ballroom dancing. You discover that you dance together without thought or concern, but the music stinks. It is time to change the music. You can choose to change it and your partner can choose to change it. Or not.

The common thread in controlling relationships is self-doubt, poor self-esteem, deep-seated feelings of inadequacy, and the need to protect ourselves from hurt, especially the hurt of rejection.

There are many forms of controlling relationships, not just the committed love relationship. How many people have worked for an obnoxious boss who seems invested in ridiculing staff members? How many have to put up with obnoxious relatives because they are afraid of causing a scene? How many people out there are getting away with mental brainwashing simply because no one challenges them? How many frightened people are out there, in how many different situations, who have discovered that the best defense may be a good offense?

Something to think about: Scratch *macho* and you find *fear* underneath every time. Test it next time you feel someone trying to belittle you or create self-doubt in you. Look beyond the actions and try to see the person underneath. Very often it's like the scene toward the end of *The Wizard of Oz*, when Dorothy looks behind the curtain and finds not a huge, frightening, powerful wizard but just a timid little man who likes to scare people. There is no reason for aggression between people other than fear. Controllers are people with fear. The fear is related to their own underlying self-doubt and sense of inadequacy. They use this self-doubt and insecurity as a weapon to gain control over others. But this is their secret and now it is out in the open; controllers are not operating from strength but from fear.

Exercise: Conducting Your Life Review—Part 2

This is a difficult exercise that will require a great deal of soul-searching and thought. It is back to the notebook. The first part of the life review was an examination of early influences. You developed it as a way of understanding how those around you influenced some of the conclusions you made about yourself. Now it is time to examine ways that you coped.

To begin, look at the conclusions you reached that fed into the belief of inadequacy and poor self-image. For example, if your father was aloof, did you try different ways to bring him closer? Did you, perhaps, try to please him without success? Did you develop the belief that, if you tried just a little harder, he would approve of you? If you were in the shadow of an older sibling, did you seek other methods of gaining attention? Did you rebel, become the "bad" one?

How did the way you interacted with others influence your opinion of yourself? Try to remember how they changed you and your image of yourself. Try to track any defensive thinking you may have developed to protect your inner self from the outside. In the notebook, you can call this section "The Shaping of My Self-Concept." Write everything down as ideas come to you. A pattern should begin to emerge. It should end with a pattern of your own unique path into self-esteem problems. This path can serve as a way back to positive self-esteem.

Next, try to define to what degree you are a Giver, Taker, Refrigerator, and Okay person. Try to rank yourself in each category on a 1–10 scale, with 1 being extremely low and 10 being extremely high. Use the descriptions in the chapter as well as the results of the pattern you have just developed to help you. You should find that some of each personality type is in you. You may find that you are foremost a Refrigerator, but quite often a Giver; at times you may be Okay and, on rare occasion, a Taker. Knowing your behavior tendencies will be helpful when it comes time to make concrete changes.

Next, try listing specific things you do that could be described as Giver behaviors, Taker behaviors, Refrigerator behaviors, and Okay behaviors. Make four separate lists. You will also find things you do to protect yourself that do not fit any of the four categories. That is good because it helps further define you as a unique person. Write down those behaviors on a separate page; later you can create your own category name to describe them.

This exercise is an ongoing work; it should not be completed in one sitting. But this initial effort is especially worthwhile because the result will be the creation of a list of specific targets for change in yourself. You will have the first stage of healing, a greater awareness of who you are.

CHAPTER THREE

How People Control
Each Other

The primary goal of a controller is to instill self-doubt in someone else. To truly understand the dynamics of control, you must look simultaneously at both the controller and the person controlled. They are completely entwined and dependent on each other. This is truly a dance between two people. Yet it does not begin at a conscious or volitional level. You do not lie awake at night plotting how to control a partner. Also, you do not lie awake at night figuring out how to be controlled. True, there are times when controlling actions can be very conscious and very deliberate. In the early stages, however, there is seldom real malice intended; it has more to do with self-protection than aggression.

The controlling relationship evolves, just like most relationships, gradually. Unfortunately, most people do not discuss and actively plan the nature of the relationship they want with a partner; they do not have periodic updates on their progress toward achieving the kind of relationship they want. Mostly, people assume that relationships just happen. They have a vague idea about what a marriage is, and they assume their partner has basically the same idea and that their relationships will just develop naturally. If things start to go wrong, they become confused; they recognize something is not working correctly and tend to blame the partner for not getting it right. They may also blame themselves, thinking they just don't get it or are truly not good enough, or smart enough, or giving enough to keep the relationship on track. There is usually no concrete set of things to do or change that you can point to, it is more like a vague feeling that something is not right, and there is often the ongoing belief that things will eventually work themselves out.

Asking Some Basic Questions

If this behavior sounds like you and your partner, you should ask yourself some basic questions. "Am I going into this relationship in a healthy way? Am I open-minded and willing to compromise and adjust? Am I set in my beliefs, thinking that if this kind of marriage was good enough for my parents, it is good enough for me? Am I married to someone who I see as my rejecting parent because I am hoping to resolve childhood issues? What preconceptions am I taking into this relationship?" Then comes the next part: "What is my partner bringing into this relationship?" All the questions you can ask about yourself must also be asked about your partner.

The suggestion that you ought to openly discuss the kind of relationship you want may seem surprising. It just is not done in our society. Couples may talk about the things they want out of life. They may dream together, have visions and try to share them, but they seldom get to the meat of things, they seem to keep it at an idealized level. Reality comes later. There is a tendency to think of commitment as a state or condition, rather than an active, evolving, and changing relationship. Only when people start to feel comfortable and sense that the relationship is locked in do they go from their best behavior to their normal behavior.

Hence the expression, "The blush is off the rose," or "The honeymoon is over." At some point after the commitment is made, reality sets in.

Questions arise: "In all the talk of romance, trips together, children and what to name them, why did you not mention that you squeeze the toothpaste tube in the middle and never put the top back on?" Or, "When I described the house I wanted, and the kind of work I did, and how I hoped our future children would all go to college, it never dawned on me that you expected me to put my dirty underwear in the hamper located all the way across the room." True, these are minor things. But there are many of them, and they can lead to criticism, bickering, disappointment, and then the ultimate in hurtful interactions—defensiveness. In different ways, walls start to go up, distance begins to form between partners.

Again, most people are on their best behavior during the early stages of a relationship. That cannot, and maybe should not, be otherwise. But you should also recognize what's going on, and expect this behavior to eventually change. If you expect it, you can face it and deal with it. Maybe you will need separate toothpaste tubes, maybe you will need to move the hamper, maybe you will even need separate bathrooms. How can you and your partner know in advance what you will need to accommodate each other? Couples learn only by discovering and discussing. You cannot change each other, you must accept each other for exactly who each of you are, accommodating those areas of difference that can cause friction. Or you will begin a dance that will lead to a power struggle and, most likely, end in either killing the relationship or forming a controlling relationship.

Negative Communication

Of course, there are other ways two people can start to turn their relationship into something negative. The important thing to realize is that it always has to do with communication, though not necessarily with words. In fact, it can even be the opposite, when a partner uses the silent treatment. It can also be little things, like the roll of the eyes in a certain way, a frown, or a look. The more subtle ways of getting a disapproving message out are just as hurtful as a direct verbal approach and they are also more clever. The message sender, if confronted, can always say, "But I never said that. You just misunderstood."

This is the typical start. Partners discover things about each other that they do not like, that bother them. The first reaction may be to let it slide, to ignore it. But, sooner or later, as irritation increases, there is a tendency to complain, to criticize. In general, the longer you choose to not deal with an issue, the more irritated you become, and the stronger your criticism will be when it finally does come out in the open. Gentleness can be lost over time.

When you are criticized, the natural tendency is to defend. "I do too put tops on toothpaste tubes." There is also a natural tendency to counterattack, "What about your underwear on the floor all the time?" Think of what happens when a person with poor self-esteem is criticized. Think of how much more powerful the defense, how much more vicious the counterattack. Gradually, two people can become invested in finding fault with each other. There can be almost a sense of victory when nailing a partner to the wall. "Gotcha that time. Just try to deny that you do this." It can turn into a real contest.

When Criticism Becomes a Control Issue

Most therapists agree that marriage problems, at heart, are communication problems. Marital problems come in many forms; couples have a wide variety of complaints and issues. But they start as communication problems and they are resolved when communication issues are addressed. If the communication style evolves into one of criticism, especially if one person is consistent in criticizing the other, the contest can develop into a control issue. Criticism, in and of itself, does not necessarily lead to control. But systematic criticism can lead to a breakdown of healthy communication and turn into a control struggle.

It is easy enough to imagine a scenario in which two people accommodate each other.

"I love peas."

"I hate peas."

"Let's make peas, but let's make another vegetable too."

Yet all too often, accommodation doesn't happen. Why? Through most of human history, marriage was perceived as a state or condition. Parents arranged marriages to acquire land or money or power. The Romans had their generals marry the daughters of conquered leaders to integrate that group into the empire. In the marriage contract, the two people were not expected to care for each other. Often times they did not even know each other before the wedding. They were just supposed to have heirs. At all levels of society, the concept of a match-maker was fairly common.

The notion of marrying by choice is relatively new. But once this concept became common, the whole nature of marriage changed. It changed from being a condition into a dynamic relationship between two people. Yet people still tend to say, "I'm married," the same way we might say, "I'm diabetic." That is, people still tend to think of marriage as a condition they have, rather than something in which they are engaged. In other words, they still tend to take the life out of marriage. At any point, however, you can try to influence the evolution of your relationship—to improve it into something closely resembling heaven, or to make it into a living hell.

What is the process of introducing self-doubt in a person? The following pages cover some of the most common controlling techniques and how they work in the hands of Givers,

Takers, Refrigerators, and Okay people. Again, these labels apply to behavior patterns; individuals can exhibit more than one type of behavior. Also there are many variations of the following control strategies. These strategies are used by controllers in general, and are not limited to any one type of person with control issues.

Basic Control Strategies

Can Givers be controllers? Yes. A common strategy for them is the solicitous comment:

Janet the Giver says to her husband Jack, "Honey, do you know what it will do to your cholesterol if you eat that burger?"

Jack snaps back. "But I want the stupid burger. It won't kill me."

Jane: "I don't understand why you are so moody and critical of everything I say. Don't you know I'm just thinking of your health? You always attack me."

There were a lot of messages in that simple exchange. The tone of Jane's initial comment is that of a parent talking to a child. What happens after a thousand, or ten thousand, such "solicitous" statements? At what point does the receiver get angry and defensive; how long does it take for a counterattack? Then comes Jack's response. It reads like a peevish child talking to a parent. It has the flavors of both defense and attack; it is emotional and skips the original health issue entirely. Although it is defensive, it cannot be defended logically. Jack has fallen into the trap of responding emotionally to a logical statement. Once he became angry, Jane gained control of the interaction. Then comes her final statement, the one designed to instill self-doubt, the coup de grace. The first line contains the accusation of insensitivity ("you are so moody and critical"), and takes the discussion from the specific to the general ("of everything I say"). That is a ploy for further argument. Jane takes the position of martyrdom and adds a justification for her solicitous comment: "I'm just thinking of your health."

The underlying theme of the Giver is always looking after the good of the other. Finally, she drives home the dagger: "You always attack me."

Think about it. Jack has just been accused of making an attack. He looks back and thinks that Jane has a point. He remembers his anger at being criticized for eating a burger—except it did not come out as criticism, it came out as caring and concern. "So if my partner is worried about me, what right do I have to get mad over it?" Jack says to himself. "I feel lessened somehow, but I can't point to anything said to make me feel that way. Am I ungrateful? Why am I feeling trapped? Why am I feeling controlled? Why can't I be allowed to eat something that is not good for me once in a while? Am I wrong? What is wrong with me?"

This was an illustration, at a very simple level, of a controlling exchange and how it can lead to self-doubt. This simple exchange between two people left one of them in doubt about his behavior. I used the example of the Giver only to demonstrate that everyone is capable of becoming a controller.

A caveat: Givers do honestly care about their partners. In fact, most people in love care about and want the best for their partners. At times, this caring can be interpreted as attempts at control when it may not be. Not every exchange like this last one is designed to enhance control. To evolve into a controlling relationship, the pattern has to be consistent, and it has to attack self-confidence by instilling self-doubt.

Withholding Approval

Takers have a very different style in developing a controlling relationship. They install self-doubt by keeping their partners off balance. The simplest way to do this is by withholding approval. Does this sound familiar? Remember, children of parents who consistently withheld approval have a strong chance of developing an inner belief of worthlessness. They also tend to enter adulthood with strong approval needs, and many of them unconsciously seek out partners who are like their parents. Often they end up with Takers who are fully equipped to continue their own childhood quest for approval—by denying it.

Givers often end up with Takers, and here is why. Givers have a tremendous need for approval from the outside, and believe they will get it if they just try hard enough, love enough, give enough. A Taker can play with this need. For example, by not quite approving, a Taker can get a Giver to try harder. By focusing on the Giver's inadequacies, mistakes, faults, failures—by staying negative—the Taker hooks the Giver. Ultimately, the Taker will make the relationship evolve to the point where the Giver is never appreciated, never complimented, never accepted. The more approval is denied, the more a Giver focuses on ways to gain acceptance—to the exclusion of any other thoughts.

This is a very important part of the art of controlling another. One can shape the focus of a partner by playing with their partner's needs. There is an old and effective approach to disciplining children that goes: Find out what they want and take it away from them. Well, if it works for children, why not for adults? If a controller can identify the needs of a partner, and deny them, it will be possible to shape the partner into a controlled person. This approach does not work if done suddenly. In fact, often the controller starts by showering the partner with the things he or she needs. This establishes a hunger for more. Whether it is love or acceptance or attention or just being taken seriously, the more the future controller provides, the more the future controlled person thinks it will go on forever. Then, when the relationship is firmly established, the controller can start to place conditions on the relationship. The bargain begins to be, "If you want this, you first have to do that."

As the Taker doles out less and less of what is needed, the Giver will try ever harder to get the reward. As this is happening, the Giver is less and less likely to examine the controller or the overall nature of the relationship. Most controlled people have some level of awareness of what is going on between themselves and their partners. But it is usually vague and not clearly defined. A Giver may have a sense that his or her partner has become mean or uncaring or insensitive or even selfish; but the Giver usually also has the idea that, if he or she just did things differently, the relationship would change back to how it was in the beginning. "I want to have the person that I married back."

Withholding is an evolutionary process. It can break your spirit if it goes far enough. It can turn a Giver into a Refrigerator.

Being Oblivious

A Refrigerator may control by becoming oblivious to the needs of a partner. There is a subtle difference between deliberately withholding approval and being oblivious to a partner. Being oblivious may be more socially acceptable than deliberately harming someone else, but it can have similar results.

In either case, the process has to be gradual—and that means there has to be consistency. If there is no pattern of behavior designed to introduce and exploit self-doubt, the partner will not join in the controlling process. Larry can forget an anniversary and not have a damaging effect on his wife Lucy, but what if he forgets every important event? Lucy will reach a point where she feels unappreciated. But Larry has simply . . . forgotten. How can Lucy get mad at that? But Lucy does get mad and try to communicate her needs. And what happens? She becomes the bad person in the relationship. "I don't understand her; she is always complaining," Larry says. "I forgot, that's all. Why does she get so upset all the time?"

Here's another example: You are going to a conference in a nice location. You get a great hotel room with a swimming pool. Meals are paid for by your company because it is a business conference. The conference ends early Friday afternoon and you have all night and Saturday morning free. You go to your room to get ready to have your partner join you for a very romantic evening. A week ago, he had promised faithfully to be there by six o'clock at the latest. At six-fifteen, while you are restlessly pacing in your room, the phone rings. You get a bad feeling in your stomach, you already know who it is. You answer the phone and the first words you hear from him are, "Guess what, I forgot."

Perhaps this has happened so often that you begin to feel unloved. You may start wondering what is wrong with you. You can easily reach the conclusion that you are just not important enough to your partner. Self-doubt can set in.

How does one deal with a person who forgets? In personal relationships, it is difficult to hold a person responsible for forgetting things, especially minor, everyday things. You always get the apology, the promise that it will not happen again and the assurance that, if your partner had only known it was so important, it would never have happened in the first place. Still you have a great feeling of rejection, of not being appreciated, of wondering if you are no longer attractive or desirable—and there is nothing you can do. Any action places you in the position of being mean and vindictive and overly demanding. It is very much a no-win situation.

Over time, frustration builds. The hurts are not forgotten and they accumulate. To avoid being hurt, you stop planning romantic weekends. Gradually, you may become what your partner has wanted all the time, another Refrigerator.

How Okay People Become Controllers

Think of the people being called Okay as those who have managed to reach adulthood reasonably unscathed by self-doubt and who are not carrying strong needs to control. But this does not imply that Okay people never become controllers. No one is immune. When a basically Okay person enters a relationship with someone who is insecure, the result can be a power struggle between the two. Power struggles are basically about control—someone will win and become the controller and someone will lose and become the controlled person. That, or the struggle will be played out over the life of the relationship with no clear winner or loser.

The Okay person who confronts a power struggle has a choice of leaving the relationship, surrendering totally, or engaging the partner in the struggle. Surprisingly, the more the Okay person loves the partner, the more the inclination will be to engage in the power struggle rather than leave or surrender to the other. Love keeps Mary from leaving and love is the element that convinces her that things can be really good if Harry and she could just resolve their relationship problems. The Okay person focuses on the healthy relationship that he or she envisions: "If I can just get you to see how great you are and how great we are together, you will be happy inside our love relationship."

Unfortunately, the "our" part of that relationship really means the Okay person's idea of a love relationship. The Okay person probably has a healthy definition of a relationship. It may be based on being equal partners, having personal space and freedom, providing mutual respect and trust, and other healthy things. But unless both partners have, or are able to adopt, basically the same definition of a normal relationship, they will still be at odds. This is not a matter of right and wrong, better or worse; it is a matter of disagreement. If the partner cannot adopt the Okay definition of normal freely and with full conviction, the partners will end up in conflict. If Harry feels inadequate to handle an equal relationship, for example, the idea of it will be frightening and he will resist it. This can easily frustrate Mary.

Remember, Mary is convinced their relationship can be healthy and fulfilling for both of them if only Harry can be convinced likewise, and to accomplish that, she tries to take control (but with only the best of intentions). That is, she chooses to engage in the power struggle with the intention of imposing the healthy relationship on Harry, "to show him how good such a relationship can be."

What the Okay person does not realize is that this engaging in a power struggle has to include the introduction of self-doubt in the partner. Here is a great irony: The Okay person wants the partner to heal, become strong and healthy, regain lost confidence—but to get there, self-doubt has to be introduced. How else can a person break down a set of defenses in a person other than by getting the person to surrender them? When there is no power struggle, it can be done with love, encouragement, and unwavering respect. But in a power struggle, the attack of the other must be countered. That can only be done by going after the other person's weapons.

For the Okay person, there is a very simple but incredibly effective tool to disarm a partner's weapons—to simply point them out whenever they are used. By identifying a control strategy a person is using, the strategy stops working. Tie that to the underlying insecurity of the partner that the strategy was used to cover in the first place, and the partner is knocked off balance. It is possible to create self-doubt by focusing on the faults and flaws of a person. Here's an example: "Honey, you're really critical today, you seem to have a real need to put me down. If you wouldn't be so insecure, we wouldn't have to go through this so often."

How does Honey answer that? Does Honey deny being critical or being insecure? It does not matter, the hook has been planted. Given enough of these mini-analyses, self-doubt will grow, and if it grows enough, power and control will move toward the Okay person.

Often the Okay person gains the very control he or she never wanted in the first place. While the goal was to create a healthy relationship, the path of the power struggle led to exactly the opposite result. The Okay person is now over-responsible, and the controlled person accepts no responsibility at all, in what becomes an adult-child–style relationship. Rather than providing the atmosphere for healing, Mary convinced Harry that there are solid grounds for feeling insecure.

The Okay person may become helpless to get out of the controlling position. Ironically, the very behaviors the Okay person is using to engage in the power struggle are the behaviors you normally think of as healthy ways of communicating honestly and directly.

There are ways to avoid this problem, however. As usual, it is less important what is said than how you say it. It is one thing to say: "You don't have to doubt me. I love you for who you are." It is quite another to say: "You act this way because you have absolutely no confidence in yourself." One expression provides acceptance without condition; the other can easily be interpreted as an attack, whether consciously meant to be or not. One expression will probably result in a feeling of reassurance while the other will probably cause either self-doubt or defensiveness. The truth is that an Okay person, or any other person, can only provide love, encouragement, respect, and affirmation to a partner. No one can make you change. Change can only come from within.

Unacceptable Behaviors

So far, focus has been on verbal ways of controlling and being controlled. But there are also a number of nonverbal tactics. The first and most common of these are unacceptable behaviors. They are clever, and it takes a certain amount of audacity to pull them off. They can range from the highly subtle to the outright obnoxious. They can be directed toward the controlled person while alone, or they can happen in front of a broader audience. A person can seem to be the nicest, most pleasant, kindest, and warmest of people in front of others, and turn into Mr. Hyde as soon as the guests are gone.

What are unacceptable behaviors? First, they are actions or words used to get a partner off balance. They are usually embarrassing to the partner and, when done in front of others, they often prompt the partner to try to cover for the controller. They are usually aggressive in nature but not necessarily openly aggressive. What they all have in common is that they go against what is generally considered to be acceptable, especially in public settings. A woman who loudly criticizes her husband in front of others; a man who tells his wife, in front of the waiter, she cannot order a specific meal at a restaurant because it is too expensive; a parent who humiliates a child in front of the child's peers; a spouse at a dinner or party not joining in the conversation and repeatedly rolling eyes and checking the time; a person appearing severely depressed while alone with a partner but the life of the party as soon as others are present—all are examples of unacceptable behavior. Often they are little things that have a big impact on the partner while catching little attention from others.

There are countless incidents of unacceptable behavior that go on all around you every day, but you hardly notice them unless you are involved in them. If noticed, they may generate a momentary thought—such as that the person is a jerk or ill-mannered—or you may have a momentary sense of sympathy for the person on the receiving end. Even when the unacceptable behavior affects you, you probably brush it aside as boorishness. You may think something like, "That is just the way he is and we have to accept him that way." After all, you cannot expect people to act other than they normally are just because they are in front of others, can you? To understand the effectiveness of an unacceptable behavior, you have to see the incident through the eyes of the intended victim. There is a very definite process taking place between two people, even if it is being played out in front of others.

Pouting in Public

A good example of someone who uses behavior as a control technique is the person who pouts at family get-togethers. This ploy is especially effective if he or she is sitting at the head of the dinner table. In one case, the controller was Paul and the controlled person was Kate, his wife. Kate recalls hosting Christmas dinner for the extended family. There were a lot of guests, and dinner preparations were hectic. Kate was doing everything she could to have a successful meal while Paul was sitting off in a corner doing nothing. As guests started to arrive and the meal was about ready, Paul started to withdraw, going off into another room and putting on the football game. Kate became agitated and worried. She felt stares and unspoken questions. What was she to do? If she went to him and asked if something was wrong the answer would be, "No, I just need a minute before we eat." This was, unfortunately, not the first time he'd behaved like this.

The meal was on the table, the guests were gathering, and out came Paul, frowning and in a funk. He was withdrawn during dinner and did not interact. He took very little food. His silence became louder than the conversation around the rest of the table. Attempts to draw him out failed; they were met with monosyllables if anything at all. Slowly the atmosphere became tense and conversation stiff and unnatural. Through it all, Kate was taking on more and more responsibility for the failing dinner. For her, the event was a disaster. She was angry at her partner, but she also blamed herself for his behavior, thinking, "If I had only been more pleasant in the morning . . ."

After the meal, in the kitchen and out of Paul's hearing, Kate has a strong investment in defending him and his actions: "He has been under so much stress lately . . ." She is afraid that, if she cannot restore good feelings and the guests leave still feeling uncomfortable, she, through association, will be thought of as a failure. No one will want to come back next time.

There are many variations on this theme. Maybe the spouse will drink too much and be too loud and insulting during the meal, maybe he will make a point of disagreeing with everything said, or maybe he will be more subtle and communicate messages only to the wife. Regardless of method, the common thread is that he behaves in unacceptable ways and gets her to accept them.

Control is accomplished by getting a person to accept unacceptable behaviors. How? By accepting the unacceptable, you compromise yourself. By covering up the actions of another, you enable the actions to happen without any consequence. By pretending the actions are acceptable or by trying to justify them, you join in the actions and participate in the control game. What results is a process that will include ever more dramatic and direct unacceptable actions.

Hidden Messages

Why would one deliberately act in unacceptable ways, especially in front of others? The answer to that question is important. Remember, there are messages passing between two people, the controller and the controlled. When an unacceptable behavior occurs in front of others, the first message is, "You see? I can get away with this, even in front of other people." This serves two purposes—to make the controlled person feel ever more helpless in the situation, and to increase the person's sense of self-doubt.

"If he can get away with this in front of others, how can I ever get anyone to see what is really happening to me?" a controlled person might think. "How can I ever get anyone to take me and the problem seriously?" Over time, the controlled person may become less likely to confide in others, either out of embarrassment or the feeling that other people think the behavior is okay. If others remain silent, out of politeness or because they do, in fact, assume that nothing is wrong, it only increases the self-doubt in the person who is controlled. "Am I really overreacting? It doesn't seem to bother the others here, why does it bother me so much? Could I be the one in the wrong?"

People who doubt themselves develop the habit of observing the reactions of others to things, and comparing them to their own reactions. They develop a kind of mental yardstick to measure how accurately and realistically they are interpreting things, especially their reactions to their controlling partners. Unfortunately, the mental yardstick is not accurate because other people may very well be restraining themselves to avoid making a scene.

The second message the controller sends is actually directed to the audience if there is one: "Being around us can turn into an uncomfortable experience." One of the controlling strategies is to isolate the controlled person as much as possible. Outside influence, especially family and friends of the controlled person, represents a threat to a controller. There is always the danger of an outsider helping the partner to recognize the controlling nature of the relationship. Unacceptable behaviors serve to drive others away. As family and friends drift away, the controlled person is ever more firmly locked into the relationship.

The third message is the deepest, most disturbing, and perhaps the most devastating of all: "You have no place to go and there is no one to help. You are alone and have nothing and no one but me." If the unacceptable behaviors work, over time the partner will begin to feel helpless and lose hope. The more the partner buys the third message, the greater becomes the almost fatalistic acceptance of the relationship—and the fewer the thoughts of getting out, of changing things.

The above is only one example of an unacceptable behavior. There have to be many spoiled dinners, combined with other incidents, happening again and again, before the messages will be heard and have the desired effect. Through it all, the controlled person has some level of awareness of what is going on, but other people will not. By the time outsiders understand what is happening, the controlled person may have very little remaining confidence in his or her judgment. This takes time, and the effect is gradual. (If he had been such a jerk the first time you took him home to meet your family, would you ever have taken him back? Would you ever have dated him again?)

Verbal Aggression

If you think of the use of controlling behaviors on an escalating scale, from bad to worse, verbal aggression comes next. Verbal aggression is a direct attack on a person, including name-calling, insults, destructive put-downs, sarcasm, jokes at someone else's expense, and any other verbal assaults designed to cut directly into a person's self-esteem. With verbal aggression, there is no mind game going on, there is no subtlety present, there is only the direct, frontal attack. This strategy can be used by anyone, especially when other controlling strategies are not working. The ultimate goal has not changed, the person is trying to introduce self-doubt.

Take the line, "If you weren't such a bitch, I wouldn't get so angry."

How could such language instill self-doubt? With consistent repetition, the unacceptable nature of the words gets lost in the struggle to understand who is causing the anger and who is in the wrong.

Before long the thinking may shift from, "Is it my fault that he's angry?" to, "I guess I am a bitch, I need to learn to tone down the things I say to him."

In fact, over time, the target of verbal aggression may adopt the same strategy and also become verbally aggressive. It is as though the target learns this new relationship language from the partner and feels it is the only way of getting through. This then gives the controller another weapon to use to develop self-doubt in the partner: "You say I have a temper and say nasty things, but just listen to yourself some time."

This goes back to the progressive nature of all the strategies, the gradual breaking down of self-esteem and the introduction of self-doubt. But, again, it only works if the unacceptable behavior is accepted. Going back to the above example, the truth is that no one is responsible for the emotions of another. There is no excuse for abusive language. You are always responsible for your actions. True, you may feel things spontaneously. Emotions are things that happen to you, not things you make happen to yourself. But you are the one who chooses the actions you will use to express or control those emotions. To get away with the argument presented in the example, the controller must first sell the notion that the partner causes the controller's behavior. Only then will the partner accept responsibility for the behavior and only then can the behaviors gradually become more and more aggressive, more and more demeaning.

There should be a standard of conduct that requires people to remain respectful of one another and to act with respect. Yes, everyone has been guilty of being impolite at one time or another. But that does not lessen the importance of working on considering the feelings of others whenever you are about to say something, especially when what you say will be in anger.

You should always remember to be polite. But just as important is the need to demand respect from those who speak to you. This means refusing to discuss things with someone who is openly insulting you or calling you degrading names. You have the obligation to yourself to defend yourself from verbal attack. It is one of the few ways you can protect your self-esteem and avoid self-doubt. If you are under verbal attack in a relationship, try to answer this question: If the other person had spoken in the beginning of the relationship the way he or she is speaking now, would you have remained in the relationship? Besides, verbal aggression can lead to physical violence; you need to stop it at the outset.

Domestic Violence

The most extreme controlling strategy is the most difficult of all to talk about, domestic violence. Physical abuse is the most brutal and direct of unacceptable control behaviors.

Most domestic violence is perpetrated by men against women, but exceptions do exist. A client had trouble controlling his anger, always seemed at the edge of a violent rage; he also had a 300-pound wife who could knock him off a bar stool at their kitchen peninsula with a single punch. There is also a great deal of physical abuse that occurs within same-sex relationships, involving both male relationships and female relationships. But the real truth is that the overwhelming majority of abuse is perpetrated by men on women, and it overwhelmingly occurs within committed relationships.

Physical abuse is most often a result of frustration, at least in its beginning stages. It usually starts to occur when other controlling strategies start to break down and the would-be controller is at a loss. If met with resistance, that person may shift from the more subtle controlling strategies to verbal aggression. From there, it is a short jump to physical violence when nothing else works. But, while on the surface what occurs is an act of violence, what is happening under the surface is actually an act of frustration and fear. One former client was a man who, in total exasperation following a long argument, threw an object at his wife's head while screaming, "If you would just do what I tell you to do, we wouldn't have marriage problems."

Often alcohol or some other substance plays a part in physical abuse. But alcohol does not cause a person to abuse another. Alcohol is a depressant, not an energizer. What alcohol does is lower the inhibition system. In a sense, it tranquilizes the conscience, which simply permits you to act on what was under the surface all along but carefully hidden from view. There is a Latin phrase, "In vino veritas." It means: With wine comes truth.

Most cases of domestic violence show a pattern of an argument building over time. The controller is facing some level of rebellion. As the argument gets out of hand, as the controller finds himself unable to regain control of the partner, frustration sets in. Both people get louder and louder. Names and insults fly back and forth. Often both parties become verbally aggressive. (Remember, the target of verbal aggression may learn to adopt the same strategy to get back at the attacker.) The controller is usually the one who will resort to violence when the shouting fails to get the message through.

Crossing the Line

Once violence begins within a relationship, there is almost an element of doom that has been introduced. The victim has only three choices: leave, get help from the outside, or accept the violence. This is a very critical moment in a person's life, especially if the victim is a woman, which is most often the case. The reason this moment is so important, the moment the first act of violence occurs, is because whatever the victim does will be reflected through the rest of the life of the relationship.

In working as a therapist with abused women, I found that most women were able to clearly remember the specific incident when their partner crossed the line physically. Some were unable to do so; those women usually said that things happened so gradually they never noticed the crossing of the line. However, none of the abuse victims had labeled themselves as victims originally. All had rationalized away the first incident, and many went through years of abuse before realizing that what was happening was actually physical abuse.

What usually happens is that the incident is somehow excused. Once the act has occurred, the abuser is immediately very apologetic, which is nearly always the case after the first incident, or first couple of incidents. There is nearly always instant concern and sorrow, and promises designed to placate the victim. Placating becomes an integral part of the abuse cycle; it is absolutely necessary in order to keep the victim off balance, confused, and willing to give the abuser another chance. Victims make up excuses: "He just pushed me." "It was more like an accident." "If I hadn't gotten him so mad, it would never have happened. . . ." And so on.

Like alcoholism, physical abuse is a progressive disease. The level of violence nearly always increases, nearly always becomes more severe. This is because violence does not get the controller what he wants; it does not kill the spirit of the victim. There will always be another confrontation, another argument that gets out of hand, another point of frustration that supposedly can only be expressed by physically lashing out.

Why would a person use physical violence against another, especially a partner in a committed relationship? To understand how the perpetrator became the way he is, we would need to examine a lot of different factors in his life; as a child he may or may not have experienced violence as the norm. In an adult relationship, however, the perpetrator is responsible for his actions, regardless of any preconception of the word *normal* or any other factors used to rationalize how one person is able to physically abuse another.

The Urge to Minimize

The victim of domestic violence has a choice but may not have identified what happened as abuse. There is a strong incentive to minimize losses; that is, to overlook the isolated incident and accept the apology. To accept the apology is more or less the same as accepting the behavior. Perhaps that is not true in the eyes of the victim, but it is almost certainly true in the eyes of the perpetrator. He has gotten away with it. If the victim allows the first incident to pass, there is almost a guarantee of a second incident, which almost guarantees a third and fourth incident and, somewhere along the way, an increase in the level of violence.

If the victim can overcome the urge to minimize, if the victim can take a definite action, then there might be a chance for change. Does this mean calling the police and filing charges? Some experts think it is important to get the incident on a police record and have a file open as a possible deterrent to future violence. Others argue that if there is a firm commitment to get outside help—marriage counseling, for example—change can begin. If the latter course of action is taken, the victim must watch diligently for any attempt by the partner to sabotage the outside help.

To be quite honest, the prognosis for change is not good. Once violence starts, the likelihood that the future holds only more of the same is frighteningly great. There is also the impact on the victim to consider. No matter how things are resolved, no matter how much healing takes place, no matter how much the perpetrator changes or how much the relationship improves—the victim will never look at the perpetrator in quite the same way. To the victim, the partner is forever a person capable of being violent to a loved one.

Sexual Coercion

Many states now recognize spousal rape as a crime, but there are few prosecutions. It is very difficult for a woman to file charges against her husband because "he wanted something I did not want." This is usually the form spousal rape takes, one person coercing the other into sexual acts that are either not wanted or are considered unacceptable or disgusting. When the sexual encounter is not wanted, and the partner insists on it taking place, control is once again in play.

You own your own body. When your partner coerces you into doing something you do not want to do, it may feel like prostitution. ("I will sell my body for a peaceful evening. If I don't do it now, I will pay for it for days.") But this is also an assault on your spirit. It is hard to look in a mirror and like what you see when you feel like a prostitute.

At the opposite end of the spectrum, sex can be used as a manipulative tool; a person can withhold sex to coerce another. Issues unresolved before bedtime can affect what happens after bedtime.

You probably think that sexual withholding is the ultimate weapon of the woman. In controlling contests, the man is usually thought of as the taker while the woman is thought of as the withholder. These strategies work even more dramatically as controlling devices, however, when you reverse the stereotypes. If the woman is more sexually demanding than the man can satisfy, she has an excellent tool with which to degrade him. She can create performance anxiety in a single night. Think of the coercive power she has just by making mild performance-problem comments in public. And a man cannot come up with a greater inducer of self-doubt in a woman than letting her know he is no longer interested in her sexually. By withholding sex, by not desiring her physically, he attacks her identity not only in terms of sexuality but also in terms of being a woman and a full partner.

In terms of control and being controlled, remember that there is a great difference between having sex and making love. If you look at your relationship, and what is going on within the sexual arena of that relationship, keeping this single thought in mind may make it easier to determine if that sexual arena has become the setting for a control struggle.

The Controller's Mental Toolshed

Controllers store the techniques they use in a mental toolshed. Think of an old-fashioned toolshed. There are any number of tools hanging on the wall. You can find various sizes of hammers, sets of screwdrivers, assorted pliers and wrenches, saws, and many other tools. When you have a project to complete, you simply select the tool or tools needed for the specific task at hand. If a nail has to be driven into a wall, you do not choose a saw to do the job; you select a hammer. You match the size of the hammer to the size of the nail. If a bolt needs to be loosened, you choose a wrench rather than a screwdriver.

Now imagine a toolshed inside your mind, a mental toolshed. It is a mental place where you assemble, organize, and store mental interventions needed to accomplish different kinds of jobs related to dealing with people. In the mind of the controller, each one of the controller's strategies are carefully sorted by category and laid out so each can be found whenever necessary. They are used without emotion or sense of responsibility for their consequences. Many times they are not used consciously, they are simply grabbed and tossed out like automatic defenses. But many times they are used consciously and with calculation. Many times they are deliberately chosen to accomplish a specific goal. In these instances, they are most often used to hurt or punish.

If the controller's partner needs to be taken down a notch, the controller may choose an insult. If the partner is getting too confident, it may be necessary to use criticism, to focus on faults, to highlight mistakes, in order to get the partner's level of self-doubt back up to where it needs to be for proper control to be maintained. If the partner becomes overtly rebellious, verbal aggression or even physical abuse may be needed.

The purpose in presenting the storehouse of controlling techniques in this way is to dramatize how coldly a particular tool can be chosen. The truth is, the actual words or acts mean nothing to the controller. Once a person being controlled discovers this truth, the power is lost. If the actual words or acts have no meaning to the controller, outside of the underlying purpose of causing a reaction in someone else, they can also have no meaning to the controlled. The hurtful things you say and do to another are only hurtful if they are believed.

Content vs. Process

It's important to be conscious of the difference between content and process. Content is what is actually being said between people. If you focus on content alone, you are stuck in the actual verbal conversation. That is, you can only deal with the things that are actually being said. But there is an entirely different way of participating in a conversation. You can focus on the process, rather than the content. To do that is like pretending you are floating on the ceiling looking down at yourself and whoever else is in the conversation and watching what is going on.

From the ceiling, you can ask questions like, "What is happening right now. What are each of us trying to accomplish?" Asking questions like that, without paying attention to the actual words being spoken, you can quickly figure out what mind game is going on. You can come up with thoughts like, "Why, he is trying to make me feel guilty; that's what is happening." You can actually see the many controlling techniques being played out.

Controlling strategies are mental games that will not work if the other person refuses to play. You cannot be controlled unless you agree to participate in the control game. The easiest way to avoid participation is to watch for specific control techniques and, once they are spotted, back away from them. Backing away consists of rejecting the actual words being spoken and not allowing them to create self-doubt. If you go through the control examples throughout this chapter, it is easy to spot the point where the controller won the game. It was when his or her words or behaviors caused the other person to experience self-doubt. Even if the message was eventually rejected, the controller won the exchange. You have to go back to the idea of control being a gradual process. You may reject the message at first but, as long as you question yourself and give credence to what is said to you, the odds are that eventually you will accept the message, and self-doubt will enter your thinking.

This section focused on the development of a controlling relationship. In it you saw both the controller and the controlled as participants in the evolution of an unhealthy relationship. All control involves the participation of both people.

A number of common controlling techniques were presented, including: solicitous comments, systematic criticism, withholding approval, obliviousness to needs, focusing on faults/mistakes, unacceptable behaviors, verbal aggression, and physical abuse; all are stored in a mental toolshed. Now it is time to analyze your own relationships in terms of these behaviors.

Exercise: Conducting Your Life Review, Part 3

This is the last part of the life review. So far you have identified those who influenced your early development and how. You have also charted the mental path you took to reach a mistaken conclusion about yourself, your nature, and your worth. Hopefully, you are seeing more clearly how you got to where you are, and that it was not a flaw in you that is the problem. It has been your attempt to interact with others, to be liked and loved, to gain approval, that led to problems inside. Now it is time to gain a clear picture of how these beliefs have affected your relationships.

You will need your notebook again. This time go back into your past and list all the serious relationships you have been in. Leave several pages for each person who was, and now is, in your life. Mark which ones ended in controlling relationships and whether you were the controller or the controlled. You may have been one or the other. Also mark the relationships that did not evolve into controlling relationships. This is important.

Starting with the relationships in which you were the controlled person, begin to analyze them. Did your partner use controlling techniques mentioned in this chapter? They are the things that made you doubt yourself and your judgment. You might also go back to the introduction and review the checklist for clues on how you have been susceptible to being controlled. Watch for patterns across relationships. Recognizing patterns of behavior is an important step on the road to change. These patterns are your blind spots, or weaknesses.

For example, suppose your father used oblivious behaviors as a control device in your parents' marriage. From watching this, you may have concluded that men are generally oblivious to their wives' needs. This, for you, is normal husband behavior. This definition of normal would carry into your own adult relationship. It could be a blind spot in your makeup. Once you see a pattern emerging, however, this kind of behavior will no longer appear normal, and you will be better able to recognize it for what it is: a control trap.

Next look at the relationships where you were the controller. List the techniques you used. More important, try to understand why you felt you had to use them. They will help point to your insecurities.

Finally, look at the relationships that did not result in control. How were they different? What did you feel toward the other person? How did the two of you treat each other? How did you handle insecurities with the other person? What ended those relationships? Take your time with this, you are creating a road map that will help you in your current relationship and any future relationships. The result should be an accurate and clear picture of you and how you deal with another person who is close to you. This will help you become much more concrete when you reach the changing stage.

CHAPTER FOUR

Life With (and Without) Control

To understand the nature of controlling relationships it is important to examine relationships that are not based on control. The differences between controlling relationships and relationships not based on control are subtle in the beginning but staggering in the shape they take.

With all the life experiences of your growing years and the years of adulthood before marriage, or getting into a committed relationship, you cannot help forming some conclusions about what such a relationship should be like. Given that everyone's experiences differ, it is very rare that two people have the same definition of what marriage is. As the differences in definitions become clear, there is a natural movement to eliminate the differences and create a single definition. How a couple goes about that evolutionary process actually does more to define the nature of the active relationship between them than the final resolution, if one is ever reached. The couple can compete with each other, or accommodate each other through cooperation. The relationship can become adversarial, or it can become a true partnership. There are many possible shapes the process can take, but the main thing is that much of what a relationship is, is the result of how the two people interact with each other rather than the final, formal definition of the relationship.

Love and the Healthy Relationship

It is not always the case, but let's begin with the assumption that most people marry because they are either in love or think they are in love with each other. Once again, people learn different definitions of the word *love* just as they learn different definitions of the other aspects of relationships—through the example of others, mixed with their own thoughts and experiences. However, in my work with couples, I have found some basic themes that, taken together, seen to define a healthy love and a healthy relationship, one not based on control. For example, there appear to be certain prerequisites for fully loving in a relationship. These include trust, respect, and being close friends.

Trusting has been defined as one person being vulnerable to another. This is a very difficult thing for someone to do. To open your heart to another is to open yourself to devastating pain if you give that trust to the wrong person. This is one of the reasons that loving fully is a process that takes time. Just overcoming the amount of risk involved in trusting another person takes time.

So, is "love at first sight" always an illusion? Not necessarily. Depending on the situation, "love at first sight" may be more accurately described as "lust at first sight," or it may take the form of an instant infatuation. But there are also those instances where two people meet and they just know they are right for each other. It is as though their spirits recognize each other. That is to say, there is no logical or earthly way to explain it, it just happens. Even those people, those who were lucky enough to "just know," go through the same process of learning to trust each other but perhaps more quickly and without the fear, uncertainty, and suspicion that others may experience.

The second prerequisite for love is respect. Most people don't pay enough attention to this fact. People tend to get too casual with each other, and with time, start to take each other for granted. After disagreements, they find it hard to maintain the same level of niceness and gentleness of the courtship period.

What is it that happens to people? Where does that niceness and gentleness go? How can people speak harshly to the person they love? How can a person be disrespectful to a loved one? What does that say of the person's definition of love?

During courtship, respect is usually mutual. It isn't until two people do things to hurt one another that they begin to act in disrespectful ways. Most often, disrespectful behavior is a method of pulling back, creating distance, and it is usually accompanied by a lessening of vulnerability. It is also a by-product of frustration, usually related to not feeling heard or understood. It represents an erosion of love. Being disrespectful is not an act of love, and it is hard to continue loving someone who is disrespectful to you. It is hard to keep loving a person who calls you names, who yells at you, who orders you to do things, or who pays scant attention to you and your needs. Without respect it is very hard to keep love alive. As with trust, partners must work at respecting each other. It is necessary to show the respect they feel to reassure each other that the love is still there.

With the loss of active respect comes indifference and personal isolation. ("I didn't tell you how I felt because I didn't want you getting mad and mean.") The biggest threat to a long-term relationship is the danger of falling into a routine that ends up with two people taking each other for granted and then slowly drifting apart. Relationships can become stale and it is the staleness that creates the perfect climate for a search for change.

The third prerequisite for love is being close friends. Can you truly love someone who is not also your friend? Some clients have told me that though they love their partners they do not really like them. These same clients have said that they feel something is missing in their relationships.

Love relationships that do not develop a strong element of friendship often do not last. When two people become involved very quickly, they may become a couple and even get married before they fully know each other; when they do get to know each other, they often find themselves unhappy in their relationship. Passion is usually the driving force in this kind of relationship, but while passion may come and go, friendship is the glue that holds relationships together. Friendship can sustain a relationship through difficult, as well as good, times. Friendship helps relationships over the long haul and through changes that are bound to occur with the passage of time.

Where Self-Esteem Comes In

To fully trust, you have to know that you are worthy of being trusted. To maintain a respectful relationship, you have to know you are worthy of respect. To be friends, you have to know you are worthy of being someone's friend. To fully love, you have to know that you are truly lovable. This is why self-esteem and feelings of adequacy are so important.

Trust, respect, close friendship and unconditional love will not happen if there is no self-love, no self-acceptance. The person who feels inadequate, the person with low self-esteem, is too concerned with the other's perceptions to fully open up. If you believe there is something really bad inside of you, you are more likely to hide your inner self than make yourself vulnerable by opening up. The first step to loving is accepting yourself as you really are. Then you can accept another as he or she really is. Remember, you are seeking the kind of love that is not part of a controlling relationship. There are many definitions of love, but most of them come with strings attached. To avoid control, the love has to be full, complete and unconditional.

The Nature of Unconditional Love

The person you love is the person you love. Start changing that person and he or she becomes someone else—and no longer the same person you love. That is why the term "unconditional love" is used. Unconditional love is loving a person exactly as he or she is, with no reservations, with no strings attached. It is knowing that you are loved in return, exactly as you are, with no reservations, with no strings attached. It is also knowing that you both deserve such love, and you simply accept it as a gift that is freely given.

The first thing you have to accept is that you are not going to change another person. You can change yourself but not someone else. The fact that you cannot change another person is one of those profound truths that people seem determined to fight. The mental process goes something like this: "I love this person overall, but there are a few things in him or her that I don't like. Once we are together, once we have committed ourselves to our relationship, I can point out those flaws and, of course, my love will recognize them as flaws and change them."

Of course, this is usually not done on the conscious, thinking level. But people sense flaws in their partners, and the very fact that they think of character traits as flaws implies that they are judging their partners using their own standard.

The odds for two people finding a perfect match in each other is about as good as winning the state lottery. There will always be areas where two people don't match. In fact, the areas where people do not match are likely to change as each person evolves as an individual. The question is what to do about those areas. You need to ask yourself the question: "Can I love this person without attaching any conditions?" You need to be able to acknowledge your differences and say, "Even though some things about you do not go well with who I am, I will love those aspects simply because they are a part of who you are." Without those aspects, your partner would be different and not the person you fell in love with in the first place.

To the person who loves, love is experienced as a feeling, but to the person who is loved, it is experienced as a series of actions. You feel love and you show love. To convey love, you have to demonstrate love, over and over, and in as many ways as possible. In that sense, you can say that the word *love* is a verb rather than a noun. What you do, how you act toward another, demonstrates how you feel about that person. If what you feel inside is love, then you will act and speak in only loving ways.

Respectful Communication

If love, as perceived by the person being loved, is a verb, and how you act is a demonstration of how you feel, then how you speak to each other is one of the clearest indicators of your feelings inside. If a person screams and yells at you, calls you awful names, orders you around, belittles you, criticizes you, consistently finds fault with you, and then, at bedtime, says, "I love you," what are you going to believe?

It is easy for two people to get into a pattern where they take each other for granted. But even when that happens, there is still no excuse for talking disrespectfully to one another. Adding an element of gentleness to your communication can avoid countless hurts that make trust and respect so difficult to maintain. In therapy, clients speak of the most horrid things they have been called or that have been said to them by people who supposedly loved them, and it is hard to understand. How do two people get to a point where communication breaks down so badly? The answer, of course, is based on the same sense of inadequacy that drives most of the control issues. If you believe you are less than your partner, you are always on guard, always protecting yourself, and always ready to counter what you perceive as an attack, whether it is a real attack or not.

You strike out at people because you are afraid or frustrated or feeling unheard. When people become emotional they stop thinking and start reacting. One hurtful reply, and the interaction degenerates into an ugly routine. Yet it is easy enough to stop. At the first sign of anger, it takes only one person to say something like, "Let's stop for a few minutes and calm down. Then we can try again." Is that so hard? The two of you can have an agreed-upon gesture to signal a need for the time-out—anything that can stop the interaction before you get so emotional that you become thoughtlessly caught up in the exchange. The mutual choice to always speak respectfully goes a long way toward removing the need for a control struggle between two people in love.

The Importance of Honesty

Besides being respectful, it is necessary to be honest about your feelings. There will be times when honesty can hurt the other person. You may feel something or perceive something that, if you voice it, will hurt the other person's feelings. What do you do? There are two possible ways to go. Choice number one: You will occasionally hurt your partner by being honest. Choice number two: You will occasionally be dishonest with your partner.

Of course, this is a trick! To have a truly loving relationship that includes mind, body, and spirit, you have to choose to be open with each other. Honesty has to do with more things than just building trust. It also has to do with learning about each other.

Everyone has sensitivities, soft spots, danger zones. You acquire them over the years through your interactions with others. Two people approach each other with only vague ideas about each other's sensitivities. You have to learn about each other, and that is usually a process of trial and error. You basically learn how to say things in ways that do not push each other's buttons. But you also have to disclose your own areas of sensitivities, and that can only be done with honest communication.

Being open about your vulnerabilities is a gift of trust. Even if being honest is initially hurtful, you will have a better relationship for it in the long run.

Accepting Differences

Imagine if two people who were perfectly matched ever did meet and form a relationship. They would be clones of each other. They could become so bored with each other that the relationship would end in no time. It is the differences that make a relationship exciting, it is the differences that provide opportunities for two people to grow.

You have a mission, which is to advance and grow as much as possible within the confines of a lifetime. What better way to accomplish maximum growth than to join with another in a growth partnership—to find someone with the qualities you need to grow, and to have the qualities your partner needs to grow?

Surprisingly, many people do this without even realizing it. Many people find others who help them to overcome a need for parental love and approval that they missed as children. A Refrigerator may find a Giver in order to open the freezer door and become a Giver. A Taker may find a Giver in order to change into a Giver. A Giver may find a Taker in order to learn to let go of a constant need for approval from others. As long as control does not enter this last scenario, it can work well.

A Taker who wants to learn how to give may meet a Giver wanting to learn how to stop being a people-pleaser and develop self-approval. The pair could make an incredibly effective team. However, as soon as one person tries to change the other, a power struggle will begin. If each person can accept that he or she is starting at different places, and have similar but not exactly the same goals, and accept that each has something to give to the other on their separate journeys, then it is possible to have a mutually helping relationship. All too often the Taker continues to take and the Giver keeps waiting for his or her turn to receive. That is to say, both remain as they were at the beginning of the relationship; both remain stuck and unfulfilled, continuing to struggle and feeling unhappy.

Can Takers ever stop being Takers? Can they actually change? The first thing necessary for anyone to change is to decide not to stay the same. Nothing can be accomplished unless a person wants to change. With the desire, any change is possible.

A note of caution. Often, people who are caught in relationships with Takers spend their lives hoping their partners will change. Do not let the above example become further grounds for sticking with a Taker who will not change. You must remember that change is difficult. Controlling people are often so invested in convincing themselves that they are not the problem—they are so consistent in blaming their partners and keeping them confused and off balance—that it is extremely difficult to admit that their problem lies within.

Still, there are ways to form positive relationships with combinations that one might think are most likely to fail. To succeed, it is important to be clear and up front about the nature of the relationship. You and your partner can create an atmosphere of growth if you actively work together.

Learning from One Another

How do you help a partner on his or her personal journey? By simply being. You help your partner by being exactly who you are as much as is humanly (hence, imperfectly) possible. You open yourself up, become vulnerable, and expose your weaknesses as well as your strengths as much as you can, and you allow your partner to grow from you. At the same time, you observe your partner who is also open and vulnerable, and you can learn from your partner what you need so that you can grow as well.

Let's take an example in which the Taker is named Jake and the Giver is Sally. In this relationship, Jake observes Sally in an attempt to open up his perspective, to stop focusing entirely on his own needs and learn to focus on the needs of others. Gradually he begins to experience the joy of giving and change begins to occur. At the same time, Sally observes Jake. In her case, when she doesn't get the feedback she wants, she learns how to give more to herself and recognize those things that she cannot really receive from another person: self-esteem, security, adequacy. Gradually she experiences the joy of self-approval and change begins to occur. Both people move to a central place. He becomes more giving while she becomes more self-assured.

If you really study this example, you can see that it is probably more difficult for an insecure Giver to grow and heal than for an insecure Taker. For the Taker, the challenge is to overcome the denial system and truly admit that the problem lies within. For the insecure Giver, there is a different challenge. The Giver is not hiding behind a denial system, the Giver is getting validation from the outside and this imitates parental approval. For the Giver, it is necessary to surrender a pattern of behavior that comes close to satisfying needs, that gives an external sense of okayness, in order to develop the more truly satisfying internal sense of okayness. This is a very difficult challenge indeed.

Mutual growth and healing can occur when two people are in a cooperative relationship rather than one based on control. Unfortunately, the norm is to enter a power struggle and either remain in a power struggle throughout the life of the relationship or evolve into a controlling relationship.

In a very real sense, the choice is between growth and stagnation. Your partner can be a vehicle for helping you evolve into the very best person you can be, or an anchor that keeps you in the same place indefinitely. It all depends on how you act toward your partner. By the same token, you can be either vehicle or anchor depending on how your partner acts toward you. The trouble is that we seldom see those alternatives as active choices that we can make. It seems that we passively, and without conscious thought, allow our relationships to evolve willy-nilly into whatever they are going to be. You need to become more aware of the nature of relationships and how they are processes that you can actively control. You need to talk about those processes with your partner, you need to give each other permission to point out when one of you is doing something to try to change the other. Only then can you get back on track toward learning instead of changing.

Note the phrase: Give permission to each other. This will help make the exchange a positive rather than a negative one. The very act of spotting a controlling act provides an opportunity for mutual growth. However, it also provides an opportunity for a power-struggle to begin. It can end in a positive discussion or an argument. All too often it goes in the negative direction.

Cooperation vs. Competition

Why do people often start a relationship so positively, with such beautiful intentions, feeling such joyful love, being so filled with one another, only to have it gradually turn negative? Why do people hurt and harm the very persons they love the most? Think again about how people learn to define what's normal to them. By observing what is going on around you, you can develop the notion that conflict is the normal state of a marital relationship. But it does not stop there. The culture itself is inundated with the concept that the sexes are caught in an endless battle.

Try this informal exercise. Take a week or two and force yourself to watch one episode of every sitcom on television, including animations. While you watch, have a notebook or piece of paper divided into two sections. Label the first section "cooperative relationship." Label the second section "competitive relationship." The task is to list sitcoms in the appropriate category. The challenge is to find any that will go into the one labeled cooperative relationship.

If you can locate a cooperative relationship on TV, it will be a first. Instead, you will probably find a preponderance of relationships composed of an adolescent male and an overly responsible female. The nature of the story line is for the male to try to get away with something or other, and for the female to outwit him with her wisdom and common sense. This is what we call comedy today. Back in the 1950s, the nature of comedy was to have an inadequate and somewhat simple housewife getting into all kinds of trouble, and for the wise husband with more common sense to come home from work at the end of the day and, in the last five minutes of the show, solve all the problems with a few clever lines.

So what is being taught? How is the culture defining marriage and relationships in general? Our sense of comedy is almost universally dependent on adversarial relationships. This is called funny, but it is also what is called normal. Competition is what children see when they are not watching their parents directly. This is what you see when you are not watching your partner directly.

The two of you have a basic choice: Do you cooperate or do you compete? The answer to that question will shape most of your interactions. It will create the atmosphere that will be the definition of the relationship. It will become the norm. It will be that which your children will use to base their earliest definition of the word *normal* when looking at marriage, father, mother, husband, wife, man, woman.

Besides your upbringing, besides other experiences, besides the so-called entertainment industry inundating you, there is also the history of your partner and your own inclination to do things the way you believe is right. All these forces are lined up to lead you toward a competitive relationship. Why? If your definition of marriage is not the same as your partner's definition, would you not try to convince your partner to abandon his or her definition and accept yours? And would your partner not do the same? The outcome depends entirely on how the two of you go about it. In trying to prove your points, there is a natural tendency toward competition and that could easily start the evolution toward a controlling relationship.

This is why talking things out, of actively taking charge, is so important. Two people can actually discuss the pros and cons of cooperation verses competition, can actively watch for competitive interactions and deal with them as they occur. Two people can create a relationship that is free of winners and losers, a relationship in which they are true equals.

Unfortunately, the women's liberation movement of the 1970s got it wrong. It magnified the competitive spirit that was already dominating male-female relationships. The feminist movement may have done something to even the playing field, but, in the end, it was still a playing field and the teams were still competing. The only solution is to get beyond the competition.

Control Mechanisms

Control through competition is actually the classic struggle for power between two people. The struggle can last through the life of the relationship, or one person can win and the other surrender, or areas of power can be staked out and shared. (One example of this would be the stereotype of the man having the power on the surface while the woman runs the show from behind the throne.) What may be most striking about the power struggle is that it is generally open and direct. People disagree, they argue, and they fight over relatively clearly defined positions. They know that they are in conflict. The fact that the power struggle exists is not in doubt. They see the situation as one that will end with a clear winner and loser.

The power struggle, however, is not the only form that control can take. Control can also take the form of restraint. In a relationship based on feelings of inadequacy, there is often a tendency to hold the partner back. This often takes the form of undermining things the partner wants to do to advance in one way or another, such as taking a class, joining a health club, taking up yoga, or making new friends outside the relationship.

The insecure person thinks: "If my partner is successful, if my partner grows and expands his or her horizons, if my partner continues with education or a profession or some other thing, eventually my partner will outgrow me, will find me so far behind that there will be no interest left in me." It may be coupled with another kind of thinking: "My partner will be out there, meeting new people, finding others with similar interests, and my partner will eventually find them more interesting than me. My partner will get bored with me."

This thinking leads to an area of control that truly is very different from the competitive area. The fear of a partner's success here is tied to a fear of loss. It is the fear of not being able to keep up. It can lead to the same sort of imprisonment that competition can create but it is more subtle than open competition. In this case, the insecure person makes it difficult for the other who is trying to advance; neither of them may recognize this process as a form of control, but that is what it is.

The controller's thought process goes something like this: "What am I supposed to do while you are taking that evening class? How do I know you are really taking a class? I think you just want to get away from me. What about all the people you are going to meet at that class? This is taking away from our time together."

If this ploy works, the partner will feel guilty. "I guess you're right, it is selfish of me to think only of what I want to learn and make of myself." The controller has used guilt to hook the partner into playing a control game. By responding to the insecurity, the partner has lost the opportunity for personal advancement and has become sidetracked into a control issue.

Joy in Each Other's Joy

What is the alternative? The answer is learning to take joy in each other's joy. Rather than trying to advance yourself through a relationship (such advancement is a personal quest), you should be trying to share in your partner's advancement. Your focus should be on the things your partner learns and takes on. It is taking pleasure in your partner's successes and developing the desire to see your partner stretch in new directions. It is the active encouragement of your partner to do new things that he or she wants to do. (Remember, you are supposed to be advancing yourself at the same time, and your partner is supposed to be enjoying your successes at the same time you are sharing those of your partner.) Each of you has to do your own advancing; it's just nice to have someone cheering you on as you move forward.

To develop this feeling demands confidence, personal confidence in your position in the relationship. If you feel unequal, inadequate, or not good enough, any success your partner experiences will feel threatening to you. You must believe in your equal place in the relationship before you can joy in your partner's joy. This may take time. It can be overwhelming to watch a partner's successes.

Whether or not you begin a relationship with a sense of confidence, once you have it, you will look at the relationship like this: "I am a valuable person. I think you are equally valuable. Together we can form something special. Of course, I want you to be everything you can be; nothing else would do because anything less would not be the person I love. I know you want the same for me. If either of us is threatened by the growth of the other, then the relationship is flawed and will not survive. I would rather keep on being me than participate in an unhealthy relationship. I do not want you to be me, I want you to be you."

Accepting Your Partner's Freedom

If you are going to keep control out of a relationship, you have to accept your partner's freedom. You can take any creature—a fly, a mouse, a fish, a parakeet, or a human being—and, as soon as you cage it, it will try to find a way out. This is the natural way of living things. All living beings want freedom; they hunger for it and thrive on it. Yes, spirits can be broken, animals can be tamed, and creatures can be born into captivity, or slavery, and be docile. But give them the dream or the taste of life as free creatures, and they will begin to change. They will grow until they try to achieve it. As a person with a partner who wants freedom, you may either try to deny that freedom and control your partner or accept that freedom and accept your own freedom as well.

There are many stories of men on baseball teams, bowling leagues, pool leagues, and card clubs, men who are out with their buddies several nights each week, who expect their wives to be home all the time and fully accountable whenever they leave to go somewhere. Sometimes people who are the most demanding of freedom are also the worst controllers of a partner's time. The opposite example is also true; there are women in clubs and groups with many time-consuming obligations who expect their husbands to be home taking care of the kids.

Can a relationship be sustained with this kind of imbalance? Probably not. True, a couple may stay together, occupying the same residence, but is there a real relationship between the partners? In examples like those above, most of the focus when the couple interacts is on complaints, on the inequity—and most of what is felt by each person is unhappiness and frustration. To get to the real underlying issues in the examples above, you have to ask the question: Why are these men and women choosing to spend most of their time away from their partners?

It is important to understand the natural need for freedom—the need to be in charge of your own life, the need to make your own decisions and choices. Each person must have this in order to flourish. The partner must decide whether to enjoy it or fight it. The choice should not be difficult because you both have exactly the same need for freedom and it is awfully hard to justify having freedom while denying it to your partner. Where does the tendency to deny freedom to another person come from? By now it should be no surprise to learn that it boils down to feelings of inadequacy. It is a frightening thing to accept the reality that a partner is a free person if you do not believe your partner wants to be with you more than anyone else in the world.

There is a special thing about freedom: It is entirely personal. You do not share freedom with another; you own it yourself. True, you can freely choose to do something with another person, but you cannot freely share the choosing. This is complex, but it is central to control. If a person is free, then a person can choose to leave you. If a person is free, you have no vote in that person's choices. If a person is free, that person owns his or her life. In a sense, you can say that person has self-control.

For someone who feels inadequate, inferior, not lovable, accepting a partner's freedom is terribly risky. That is because there is really nothing you can do to influence the choices of a truly free person. On the other hand, there is no higher compliment, and there is nothing more valuable, than being loved by a completely free person. In this case, love is a choice that is freely given. If there are no strings attached to love, if there is no control brought into play, then the person loved can feel true security with a partner. Then all the things talked about so far, trust and total intimacy, can happen.

The Real Meaning of Intimacy

Intimacy can be thought of as a spiritual connection between two partners. It can happen at a number of levels. It can be nothing more than a touch of fingertips, or it can reach an immeasurable intensity of passion. It is a communication without words. It is a reassurance of being loved. Intimacy can take many forms: a picnic on a beach, listening to music while lying together on the living room floor, dancing together, quiet and attentive conversation, a voluntary back rub, cuddling on a couch, a rose in a bud vase sent unexpectedly. Most often, perhaps, intimacy is something that goes on as people gaze into each other's eyes.

Intimacy is most needed during or shortly after periods of stress and at times when one feels insecure. The more insecure a person feels within a relationship, the more the need for intimacy. But that does not mean that fully secure people do not need intimacy as well.

There are also people who are strongly locked into their personal freedom and who carefully guard and protect it. They think in terms of choices throughout every day. They value their self-control and they exercise their freedom. For them, intimacy is the way of reaffirming the choice to stay in the relationship. There is an interesting comparison here. For the insecure person, there is a strong need to receive intimacy as a way of reaffirming that he or she is loved by the partner. For the secure person, there is a strong need to give intimacy as a means of reaffirming that he or she still loves the partner. When both people feel insecure in a relationship, they are both measuring the amount of intimacy they receive and comparing it to the amount of intimacy they give. They become dissatisfied when they are not receiving at least as much as they give. With two secure persons who are confident in their relationship, it is more a matter of each person feeling the importance of giving intimate messages as often and as lovingly as possible to continue to show their feelings.

There is an element of intimacy in all relationships, with boundaries that are appropriate for the particular relationship. Among acquaintances, it can be a handshake. Even with business partners intimacy exists, perhaps in the form of scheduling the next meeting together. In marriage it has no boundaries because marriage is so complete and total a relationship.

Intimacy, like love itself, works better when it is freely given rather than expected. This goes back to the question of control. How can intimacy be part of control? True intimacy, freely given, in and of itself, is not part of a control system. But even intimacy can be distorted and subverted. Withholding intimacy until certain conditions are met is a great way of controlling another person. Moreover, what is eventually delivered will not really be intimacy, it will be payment for services rendered. However, rejecting the intimacy offered by another is an even more effective method of control. Refusing a partner's message of love until certain conditions are met is not much different from rejecting love itself; it can be crushingly painful. The acceptance later is not a participation in intimacy; it is an acknowledgment of control.

But there is another issue here. If a person truly does not want to accept or send a message of love, an expression of intimacy, it would be dishonest to do so. It is not the refusal to send or reject that leads to control, it is subjecting the expression to certain conditions. One must be honest in a relationship and there are times one honestly feels uncomfortable with intimacy. It should be discussed and resolved, of course, but it has to be accepted that not everyone is always receptive to intimate expressions.

What's most important is staying honest and responding naturally.

Love, Sex, and Control

In any sexual relationship, there is a difference between having sex and making love—and it's important to avoid confusing the two. In a deeply committed relationship, making love is an affirmation of the deep bond you share.

This is not to say that you should strive to make love with your partner every time you are intimate. Sometimes you may prefer the purely physical—and less demanding—experience of having sex. What's important here is that what you choose to do together is mutual.

It is hard to think of making love in a context that includes control. You just cannot use making love to get something from your partner. However, the same is not true about having sex. Giving, or withholding, sex from a partner is an age-old control method. Another therapist once said, "What married person hasn't been a prostitute at one time or another?" She may have been right. There is no more powerful tool to control another than the use of your own body. It is the same for demanding sex from a partner who is not in the mood. It is a control device. "Give me what I want or suffer the consequences." The consequences may be nothing more than withdrawal and pouting until the partner gives in, or it may be more serious than that. Regardless of the form, it is all control.

While demanding or withholding sex from a partner may be an effective way of controlling, it is also something almost guaranteed to kill the love between people. It turns the act of loving into a business arrangement to be negotiated. This takes the spontaneity and naturalness away from it.

When one person wants something that the other is not comfortable doing, a potential for a problem between the two people can develop. It can be resolved several ways. On the one hand, a person in love does not want a partner to be uncomfortable and may forego whatever it was that was desired. On the other hand, a person in love may choose to stretch the limits of comfort to please a partner, and so agree to do something he or she really does not want to do. These are natural solutions that involve free choice. As long as it remains a free give-and-take, it is still loving. However, if there is a price involved, either an expected reward for the performance of the act or anticipated punishment for not performing the act, the physical expression of love has been reduced to a business proposition. Control is introduced and it is killing real love.

Evolving Together

Being able to evolve with someone else may be the most important factor in a long-term relationship. It may not be easy.

People are beings in the process of becoming and evolving. The very act of living is an evolutionary process. You change, you grow, you learn, you experience, and you remember the experiences. Nothing about life is static.

Evolving together can be complicated or quite simple. The most you can hope for is to have your path run parallel to that of the person you love. But it is much more likely that the path you follow will take twists and turns that move close to, and then away from your partner. This is where taking joying in each other's joy and accepting each other's differences become so important.

You can share your personal evolution with your partner. You can do this in several ways. You can talk about where you are going and what you hope to accomplish. You can also watch your partner evolve and become an ever better person. Your paths do not have to mirror each other. Just as you are trying to achieve your highest potential, your life purpose, your partner is trying to do the same thing. But your partner is not trying to accomplish your life purpose; your partner is trying to accomplish his or her own life purpose.

Personal evolution is like freedom in that it does not happen in conjunction with another, it is done alone. Another person can watch you evolve, and even cheer you on as you move forward, or feel badly if you stumble. But no one else can participate in your process of evolving.

To watch a partner, a loved one, evolve takes confidence. With insecurity, you would constantly wonder if your partner will evolve away from you, find someone else with more in common, and finally leave. With insecurity, you may be tempted to hinder the evolution of your partner and stop any progress. You may want to keep your partner in exactly the same place where you are, in order to ensure that you stay together.

To fight another person's evolution, or advancement, is about the worst crime one person can commit against another. It is, in essence, trying to destroy another person's identity. It is the stopping of growth, the destroying of all dreams and hopes; it is taking away a future.

Parenting as a Team Effort

Parenting offers you the opportunity to help the next generation be all it can be. No matter whether two people do well or poorly as parents, what they do is done as a team. When working with parents, one therapeutic approach is to get them to always ask themselves and each other the question: "What am I teaching?" Parents do many things, but teaching is the single thing parents do most. Almost everything an infant and toddler learns is through observation of the parents. Also, the deepest lessons you carry through life are those that are learned at the earliest part of life. It is like being born with very plastic minds that gradually harden and set as the years pass. The younger the person, the softer the plastic. The softer the plastic, the deeper the lessons will sink.

What do parents teach children? If two people are locked in a power struggle, if they are in a controlling relationship, if they compete with each other, if they focus only on meeting their own needs and do not worry about the needs of others, this experience is what they teach. That is what life in a relationship is like to the children. If the two people take being a team seriously, if they coordinate their parenting, if they send consistent messages, if rules and punishments are clear, if they back each other up on decisions, then this is the example they set. That is what children learn about life in a relationship.

In this, there are no excuses. Parents are responsible to and for the next generation. No matter what your upbringing may have included, you have the power to influence what comes next. That is a sacred duty. If your start was bad, you can break the generational chain. If you had a good beginning, you can pass that on. The same is true of your partner. That is why discussing parenting together is so important. Yet many partners simply parent, with no plan or coordination between them. By not coordinating and planning, there is fertile ground for competition over the children, which goes right back to the issue of control.

Some Practical Advice for Parents

It's easy to come up with at least three commandments for parents. First, whoever speaks first is right. Second, don't ever disagree in front of the children. Third, get the rules and punishments down in writing and preferably taped to the refrigerator door.

When one parent overrides the other parent, what does the other feel? Hurt, rejected, unparented! That can start a resentment which can lead to a retaliation, and you are suddenly back on the road that leads to control. One parent may not agree with the other in a particular instance, but it is more important to allow the other to be a parent than it is to win an encounter. If a child can get parents to argue over a parenting issue, the door for manipulation has been opened for the child. Children quickly learn how to play one parent against the other. Not only have you taught the child how to manipulate people, you have parents in a power struggle with control not far away.

Much of the room for disagreements can be eliminated by having rules and punishments already agreed upon and in writing. If rule number four is no talking back, and the punishment is ten minutes in the bathroom, when the child talks back, there is no need for discussion. The alternative, so often, is parents ending up arguing over the severity of infractions as they occur and the severity of punishments as they need to be handed out. In this kind of process, it is easy to destroy the healthy process of raising children, a process that is supposed to be so beautiful and fulfilling.

Summary: Creating a Balanced Relationship

Given how easily it seems that control can slip into a relationship, you may think it is a wonder that there actually are committed relationships that are not based on control. In those relationships, the dominating theme seems always to come down to feeling self-confident within the relationship. It is the perception of inadequacy that usually leads to conflict and competition, and this ends in control or an ongoing struggle for control.

As long as the focus of two people in a relationship is on each other and the actions of each person are designed to celebrate the other person, the relationship can usually remain free from control issues. Likewise, if you focus on yourself, on your needs and not your partner's needs, a competition is likely to start, a power struggle is likely to develop, and control is likely to be the end result.

This also explains why it is so important to have a balanced relationship. You can best be focused on the well-being of your partner if you know that your partner is focused on your well-being. You are equally looking out for each other. You can best celebrate your partner because you know that your partner is celebrating you. Your actions can best be designed to give pleasure and satisfaction to your partner because you know your partner is focused on doing things that give pleasure and satisfaction to you. But if you lose the balance, if the relationship becomes unequal, all is suddenly at risk. One person cannot help noticing if there is consistently more giving than receiving. It is human nature to start keeping score; and a decision to keep score, by definition, is the first step toward a competition.

Life with or without control: to maintain a healthy relationship, you make the choice all the time. You need to train yourself to watch for moments of weakness, for hurts and misunderstandings, for miscommunications, for false assumptions. You must give and accept permission to discuss everything that bothers you or about which you feel uncertain. A relationship free from control is hard work to maintain, but is it not evident that the rewards of such a loving relationship far outweigh the effort it takes to achieve it?

Exercise: Analyzing Your Relationship

This exercise is designed to assess your relationship with your partner using the criteria for a healthy relationship presented in this chapter. You will need your notebook for this. Before starting, go back to part 3 of your life review, where you analyzed your role in relationships. Did you include your current relationship in that exercise? If so, you can refer to it as we proceed.

One of the basic elements of a healthy relationship is trust. Thinking in terms of trust, try to write down things about your relationship that either point toward trust or toward a lack of trust. If you need examples, go to the checklist in the introduction. Does your partner trust you? Is your time away from your partner tightly controlled? Does your partner accuse you of doing things behind your partner's back? You can reverse the questions. Do you trust your partner?

Now move on to the next criteria: respect. Think about how you and your partner interact. Try to describe things that illustrate the presence or absence of respect in the relationship. Does your partner put you down, either when it is just the two of you or when you are in public? Are your ideas discounted without reason? Again, reverse the questions, and ask yourself if you respect your partner.

Now look at the degree of friendship between you. Does your partner try to avoid being with you? Do you avoid being with your partner? Do you have fun together? Are you and your partner friends?

Using this same method, move onto the other criteria for a healthy committed relationship, including unconditional love; respectful communication; ability to accept each other's differences; ability to learn from each other; ability to cooperate; intimacy and sex. Ask yourself these questions: Does your partner expect you to agree with him or her all the time? Does your partner respect your ideas? When talking about things that matter to you, do you feel heard? Are you happy with the level of intimacy in the relationship?

When you examine the degree of cooperation in the relationship, you need to look at the degree to which you work together to solve problems; the degree to which you are able to find a middle ground. On the facing page, you may want to create a separate category for "competition," which is the opposite of cooperation. To what degree does your partner compete with you? Does your partner see conflict as a competition? Does he or she always have to win? Remember to reverse all of these questions, asking yourself how you deal with conflict, and so on.

Now, look at how you and your partner are evolving as individuals. Do you have the freedom to be yourself? Finally, if you have children, evaluate the partnership as a parenting team. Are you harmonious or at odds with each other?

This exercise should give you a clearer picture of the dynamics of your relationship. If you are in a controlling relationship, this exercise should also help you clarify the issues. If you want to improve your relationship, it can serve as one half of a foundation for change. If your partner is willing to do the same exercise, you will each have a well-developed list of issues on which to work. How to work on improving your relationship will be covered more fully in chapter 6.

CHAPTER FIVE

Change Begins on the Inside

It is now time to look at the real person that is inside you and, if you are being controlled, to look at how to change your life. The first step is accepting who you really are.

The You Inside of You

There is something very important inside every individual. It is the essence of who you are, your identity. Knowing, understanding, and accepting your inner self is essential to regaining your freedom.

How many times have you felt that you do not know yourself? It is a common feeling. People do things and then look at their actions and say, "I can't believe I did that." People feel confused about themselves at times. Yet there are other times when people feel so fully in tune with themselves that they question nothing. There are times of inner harmony and other times of feeling totally scattered.

As a culture, we do not focus on connecting with our inner selves, which may be part of the problem. Society is generally more external in its focus; you are judged on how you influence things outside of yourself. People understand that landing a bonus or a raise is an achievement, but they may not see that having an evening filled with inner serenity is also an achievement.

How Mistaken Beliefs Happen

Your inner self is the center of who you are. Unfortunately, the mind is not perfect. The mind is only as good as the information contained in it. If some of the information is faulty, it can affect the inner self's attempt to interact with the outside. You may strive for good things and find that your attempts are not successful; you may have good intentions but poor results. This actually has a lot to do with the things that you learned to believe were real and true.

One of the things discussed in the first chapter was the idea that the human mind, at birth, has some things already built into it. It knows how to operate the heart and the respiratory system and various other things. It also has some predispositions already there. But the pool of knowledge, the process of thinking, the sorting through of data and experiences, is blank at birth. Over time, you may learn that the only way to feel loved is to please and appease or that feeling things like love can lead to the pain of rejection. You take in this information and learn to cope.

People sometimes speak of having a voice inside of them. In truth there are several voices representing parents, partners, siblings, and anyone else with influence over you. You have to be careful whose voice you are listening to at any given moment. The problem is that your inner voices all sound very much alike when you listen to them. At times, you may think you are listening to yourself when you are actually listening to your father or mother or someone else. Over time you can develop a tendency to accept other people's beliefs as your own.

If there are faulty beliefs buried in the "software" of the brain, mistakes in logic can happen. For example, you may be following a logical process, trying to figure out how to do something, and you may be doing fine until the process runs across the belief that you cannot do anything right. The logical process will incorporate that false belief and come to the conclusion that you cannot do what you were trying to do. The inner voice will say, "Sorry, can't be done."

With time, attention, and a critical awareness, you can learn to tell when a false assumption is being pushed into your thoughts or when you are really connected with your own inner self and can trust your thoughts. Sometimes an outsider may be better able to spot inconsistencies and contradictions in your self-talk than you are. This is why outside help, such as a therapist, may, at times, be beneficial.

Actively Fighting the Mistaken Beliefs

You are not the helpless product of your upbringing. You always have the choice to change. How many times have you been about to do something and gotten the feeling inside that something is not quite right? It is almost like a warning sign to change course or do something differently. People get these "warnings" and may have no idea where they are coming from, but you can learn to trust them. It's your intuition telling you something important. It seems that the more people trust these messages and listen for them, the more often they are heard. These messages are from somewhere deep inside and are bypassing sometimes faulty programming.

The other thing you can do is teach yourself. You can learn new tricks. You can read books and articles, you can take classes in different subjects, and you can slow down enough to consciously think through problems and resolve them on your own. All these are tools you can use to clear away mistaken beliefs and allow yourself better access to what you need to accomplish your goals.

Exercise: Finding Your Mistaken Beliefs

This exercise is a way of building on the work you did in part 1 of the life review. In that exercise you saw the development of mistaken conclusions about who you are and what value you have. This exercise is designed to help you locate the language that keeps those conclusions alive. Remember, as in the previous exercises, identifying any deeply set pattern within your makeup takes time. As with the previous exercises, it is best to not try to complete it in one sitting.

Mistaken beliefs often reach the surface as negative thoughts about yourself. These are thoughts that pass quickly and almost unconsciously through your mind during the course of a day. The purpose of the exercise is to become actively aware of these thoughts and then to analyze them to uncover their underlying meaning.

For at least two weeks, carry your notebook with you wherever you go, and try to write down your negative self-thoughts as they arise. This will get easier with practice. If you repeat a negative thought, make a note of it. You may find common words emerge as a pattern. For example, you may call yourself stupid, or think something you did was stupid, or say, "That was a stupid idea," repeatedly. The more times you repeat a negative thought, the stronger is the underlying mistaken belief.

Later, perhaps in the evening when you have quiet time, look at the list. Each statement says something about how you see yourself. Where did the thought come from? For example, if you continually say, "That was stupid of me," it means you do not trust your intelligence. How did that belief get there? Was there someone in your life who consistently criticized you? What other patterns are there? How did they get there?

Go back to your life review. Look for patterns in how people influenced you, look at how you adapted to them, look at the conclusions you reached. If you think about it enough, you will find the answers. This will help clear up the mystery of your mistaken beliefs and make clearer what is mistaken about them.

What It Means to Be Free

The importance of freedom in a relationship is clear. But freedom is as much a perception as it is an actual state of existence. A great thinker, named Victor Frankl, speaking from the confines of a concentration camp, said that the last of our freedoms is our own attitude in any given set of circumstances. You can be free inside a high security prison, and you can be imprisoned in the widest of open spaces. It all depends on your perception and your attitude.

But that does not mean you can close your eyes to the real world. You can be free inside that high security prison, but you must also open your eyes occasionally and see the walls. You may define freedom any way you want, but whether or not you are truly free depends on how well that definition corresponds to the real world around you.

Suppose you decide that freedom means being able to possess anything you want any time you want it. So you are walking down the street and see a Mercedes-Benz parked at the curb with keys inside. Are you free to take possession of the car? According to your definition of freedom, the answer is yes. According to the policeman on the corner watching you, the answer for you is, perhaps, five years in a high security prison.

Exercise: Finding Your Own Definition of Freedom

This exercise will help you develop a unique definition of freedom, one that you can live with and that fits your situation.

Look at your life situation. Make a list of your responsibilities (at work, home, financial, interpersonal, parenting, and so on). Make a list of the expectations of those around you. The list may include spouse, children, employer, and others who have influence over your life. The list can include preparing meals to a certain schedule, driving children to sporting events, working overtime when necessary—anything that is expected of you by others in your life. These lists represent your current boundaries.

After looking carefully at the lists, the first question is: What space is left over? What freedom do you already have? List those areas: an evening away from the family, with friends or other relatives; a sports league; reading time; sleeping in on Saturday mornings; anything that can be described as time or activities belonging solely to you. The second question is: Within the current boundaries, what is not reasonable? What is unacceptable? Where can you make more space for yourself?

The answers to these two questions will evolve into your definition of freedom. The final question is: Can I be happy within this definition of freedom, or do I have to make drastic changes?

Putting It All Together

Once you know how to listen to your inner self, you will see how essential it is to feel free in a relationship. Being free is essential to your personal evolution. You have to be able to make your own decisions, to learn and grow in ways that will lead to your unique fulfillment. Anything less is compromise.

What does compromise mean? Different people will have different definitions, depending on their perspective, but it really means giving up something to get something else. Take a man who was accused of a crime he did not commit. His lawyer wanted to work out a plea bargain that would result in a minimum time in prison. But the man was innocent, so he refused to give up a part of his life in order to avoid taking the chance of losing a greater part of his life if a jury found him guilty. The lawyer considered his client uncooperative for not accepting what the lawyer considered a good deal. The lawyer thought the compromise was gaining something—a lesser sentence. The man saw the compromise as a terrible loss: time in prison and a criminal record when, in fact, he was innocent.

But what happens when you compromise yourself? It means you give up something of yourself. Depending on your perspective, you may see it as a gain because the compromise may contain an acceptable trade-off. But you are nevertheless surrendering a part of yourself. You may choose to do this. Ultimately, however, there is only so much of yourself to give away. What happens when there is nothing left to give? You have, in essence, lost yourself, given yourself away.

In controlling relationships, remember, it's not about two people negotiating with each other and finding accommodating solutions to disagreements. I am not talking here about normal day-to-day accommodations. The latter do not involve giving yourself away. I am talking about surrendering control over your life to another person. If you turn the power of choice over to another, you have given away a piece of your self.

Controlling relationships are where most self-compromises occur. The controlled person is constantly making personal compromises, surrendering rights and power—to keep the peace, to avoid conflict, to avoid rejection, and so on. But the controller is also making personal compromises—the controller is just as unhappy as the controlled partner. The controller is just as invested in keeping the peace, avoiding conflict, and especially avoiding rejection. The controller is stuck with the rights and the power. Imagine a prisoner who is so dangerous he needs twenty-four hour observation; if a guard must watch that prisoner all the time, then is he any less a prisoner? The answer, of course, is that the two are locked together. Neither are free.

Exercise: Identifying Your Self-Compromises

This is another awareness exercise. It is designed to give you more clearly defined areas that need to change if you are going to end the control in a relationship. When someone makes a demand of you that you do not want to accommodate, but you end up agreeing to it anyway, you have compromised yourself. Make a note of the compromise, the person you gave in to, and how much giving in bothered you (you can use a scale of 1 to 10). Start keeping a list of you self-compromises as they occur.

Look at the relationship assessment exercise at the end of chapter 4. Does your partner force you to compromise? Who chooses the TV show that you watch? Who picks the movies? Who decides when it is time for sex? Look at the other people in your life. Does your boss get you to do things beyond your job description? Are you the one usually picked to work late or come in on a Saturday?

Do this for two weeks. If you make the same compromises again, make a note of it. Later, go over the list. As in the other exercises, look for patterns. Do some people have more control over you than others? Do you compromise with nearly every-one in your life? Raising the awareness of your patterns will help you combat it in the future. It will also show areas of weakness that you will need to work on.

Your Importance As a Person

Who is to say that one person's reason for existing is more important than another's? Any two people have equal value. It is just that most people do not believe this when it comes to themselves.

You were born with confidence and a natural acceptance of your worth and value. You have to be taught to feel inade-quate; you have to be taught to have low self-esteem. It is brainwashing plain and simple. But you can reverse the brain-washing. You have to teach yourself your value all over again.

It is an act of faith. It is saying, "I know I am valuable simply because I know it."

Believing in yourself is truly an act of faith. You have nowhere to go to have your worth proven to you. You either believe it is there or you do not. When you have been rejected, when you have been belittled and criticized for so many things, when you have been taught that you can do no right, it becomes very easy to lose faith in yourself.

The challenge is to break through what may be years, what may be a lifetime, of one outlook. The challenge is to attack the belief that there is something wrong with you and you are just not good enough to measure up to the rest of the people around you. You must go back to the original outlook you had. You were born believing in yourself and you can retake control of your life by regaining your original vision of yourself.

This will take time and concentration. Don't expect a quick fix. If you hear the message, "You are okay. Now that you know you are okay, let us move on to the next issue," stop right there. Your response should be: "Whoa, too much to swallow in one sentence! Tell me more about how I suddenly got to be okay. I have too many reasons to not feel okay."

Taking Yourself Back Without Getting Angry

In the process of regaining self-acceptance, you may find yourself getting angry at people in your past. As you begin to see how others influenced you in negative ways, you may want to blame them. This would be a mistake for several reasons.

Remember people, by and large, are not deliberately trying to damage other people. This is especially true of parents. To understand the errors or shortcomings of your parents, you would need to understand how your parents got to be the way they were by the time they started raising children. Yes, there are evil people out there, and there are people who deliberately and consciously set out to control others by tearing down self-esteem, but even they got to where they are through some kind of process. This is not an excuse; every person is responsible for everything they do and for the consequences of their actions.

There is, however, a more central reason to avoid negative feelings toward others. If anger, resentment, ill will, even hatred, is what you carry inside of you, then anger, resentment, ill will, and hatred are the things that will live and grow inside of you. Why carry these feelings around when you do not have to do so? They will only hinder your advancement and progress. You are not going to find inner peace with these negative emotions inside. They will serve as arguments that you are not okay.

There is a great difference between being a person who can get angry over something and being an angry person. The goal is not to judge or blame or think of revenge. The goal is to achieve understanding. In order to let go of your mistaken beliefs about your value as a person, you must first understand how you formed those beliefs, where they came from and who taught them to you. Only then can you move beyond them.

Resisting Self-Sabotage

Getting past mistaken beliefs will not be easy, but the life review you prepared earlier is the vehicle to make it happen. You need to fight self-doubt at this point. You may discover that your own resistance to change is powerful. Remember that you have learned to survive in the control environment. Change means stepping into the world of the big question mark. The more adept you are at surviving in the world of control, the more difficult it may be to break free.

For most people, achieving understanding is truly enough to be able to discard the feeling of inadequacy and develop a more accurate assessment of their okayness. The secret seems to be in making sense of it. Use your life review to accomplish this. Go over it as often as necessary until you truly see how a process of events you did not understand at the time affected your confidence in yourself.

Thinking Your Way Out of Feeling Inadequate

As you work on all of this, remember that there is another reason why you can think your way out of feeling inadequate: It was you who thought your way into the false belief! This is not about gaining a new sense of self. This is not about adopting a new way of looking at who you are. It is even true to say that this is not about creating a new sense of worth and value. All along, it has been about returning to your original conviction that you are valuable.

This concept is crucial. The change is not a step forward, it is a step back to where you began. That is why it is a rethinking process. If you were able to surrender a correct belief about yourself and accept an incorrect one, you can surrender the incorrect view of your worth and recapture your original belief, which is that you are a valuable person. Since you began life believing in yourself, then that belief is in you somewhere just waiting to be reawakened.

Many of the choices you make in life are based on your perception of yourself. If you can return to the innocent belief that you are not inadequate, you will maintain a healthier belief system and consistently make better choices.

No Longer Accepting the Unacceptable

The next step, after truly understanding that you are a valuable person with rights, is to retake control of your life. If you are to be free, you have to be in charge of what happens to you. How do you do that? The first thing to do is determine what is acceptable to you and what is not. You have to stop accepting unacceptable behaviors. As has been the case all along, this principle applies to all relationships, but nowhere is it more important than in a committed love relationship.

As noted often before, the process of moving from the blind honeymoon state to what is real, and then sometimes onward toward the unacceptable, is a gradual one in a relationship. One consequence of the gradual nature of the process is that by the time you realize your relationship is now based on control, you may end up feeling guilty for trying to change things and get the relationship back to where it was when it was good. It's as though you are the one who is breaking the agreement on what is acceptable and what is not.

It may, at first, be difficult to recognize just how controlled you have become. And yes, in a way, to want changes is breaking the agreement of what was "acceptable." However, with awareness you gain the power, and you have always had the right, to rethink things. "What was acceptable while I was under your control is no longer acceptable to me now that I understand what is really going on," you must insist.

Is that really allowed? Is it really okay to ask to change the contract? Well, are you allowed to evolve? Are you allowed to learn, and then grow from what you learn? If the evolutionary process, the learning and growth process, is supposed to last only from birth to marriage, and then stop, what would be the purpose of living beyond your wedding day? You are not here to stagnate, not at any point of your life. You are here to evolve, which includes gaining insight in all areas of your life but especially in your relationships, in how you interact with other people—and there is no more profound interaction than a marriage.

At the end of chapter 4, you reviewed the elements of your relationship with your partner. Now it is time to examine all the aspects of that relationship and decide for yourself what is acceptable and what is not acceptable. In a sense, you redesign the relationship into what you want it to be. It becomes your point of negotiation if the two of you decide to change it.

You will need a clear vision of the life you want to lead, including how you want to lead it, within a committed relationship.

Now comes the big question: Is the life you described for yourself possible within your current relationship? You may not be able to answer that on your own, you may have to bring your partner in on this part. But, even with your partner's input, the decision concerning what you do next is your own personal decision. You will have to make the decision on your own.

Exercise: Identifying the Unacceptable Behaviors in Your Life

This exercise is designed to take the mystery out of the patterns in your relationship. Again it's a matter of paying greater attention to unacceptable behaviors.

When your partner does something that you feel is unacceptable, but you do nothing about it, get out your notebook and write down the incident. If there are repeat incidents, it is important to note them because they identify the more serious problem areas. If you have trouble recognizing when you accept the unacceptable, go back to chapter 3 for guidance. You can also use the information developed in previous exercises to help.

It will also help if you keep a record of when you allow other people to act toward you in unacceptable ways.

There are several patterns you are trying to identify: the people who have the most control over your freedom, the areas where you feel least secure, perhaps also areas where you feel confident and willing to assert yourself. You may find your partner gets you to accept the unacceptable and no one else has that power. You may find that you give in only in personal relationship situations but you can be very assertive at work. Write down any pattern you recognize as you see it emerge. This will help you identify areas to work on.

Fighting Against Self-Compromise

The idea of compromising yourself has been presented a number of times. With each self-compromise, people give away a piece of who they are. The good news is that it is always possible to take your self back. It is not as though you go around with a little hatchet and, when someone wants a part of you, you chop off a finger, or a foot, and give it away. It is a mental process, and it can be reversed.

Mentally, you surrender a right or a behavior or an amount of personal power to another. Maybe you give up the right to have a say in family expenses. Maybe you give up ownership of your body by surrendering the right to refuse unwanted sexual demands. Maybe you give up the right to decide where to go on vacations. Maybe you simply give up the right to use the television clicker. That is, "If I turn on the show I want to watch, I'll spend the evening with a grouchy face, so I'll just skip it." And so on. To compromise yourself is to give yourself away—piece by piece.

Yet at any moment in time you can take it all back. You can cancel the agreements and no longer surrender. Self-compromises are ongoing processes, which is why they are so damaging to the self-esteem of the compromiser. Every time the controller makes a demand, it requires a new surrender. For example, you do not simply agree across the board to have sex every time your partner wants it; you surrender your body each time you agree to do something you do not want to do. You do not sign away total control of the television clicker; every time you want to watch a show your partner does not want to watch, you have to surrender the clicker.

By the same token, however, at any time you can choose to take yourself back by refusing the demand. It takes a decision, willpower, and an action. Nothing more. Well, maybe that is already plenty.

Again, there are times you choose to do something you do not particularly want to do, simply because you want to please your partner. To qualify as a self-compromise, it must be the surrendering of a piece of your self; some kind of coercion must be involved. It is a control interaction. Furthermore, this change should not mean rigidly guarding each and every right you have. You don't want to get into a power struggle, but rather you want to leave the old control games behind.

Will it be easy to take yourself back? No, but it can be done. The longer you have been making self-compromises, the more difficult it will be to break the patterns. Will it cause problems within the relationship? Most likely, and, again, the longer it has been happening, the worse things will be.

How Control Operates in Cycles

In any controlling relationship, conflict tends to resolve itself in a cyclical manner. In fact, since two people are involved, there are actually two cycles of behavior here that fit together.

Here's an example of how one such dynamic works: The controlled person experiences a rising sense of dissatisfaction and becomes determined to leave the relationship. Meanwhile, the controller experiences rising tension and insecurity. He or she explodes (in an attempt to regain control), and then tries to do damage control (in a further attempt to regain control). The controlled partner's determination to leave erodes in response to fears of the unknown. He or she reassesses the relationship, goes into denial, and experiences a change of heart. A honeymoon period follows for both, followed by growing dissatisfaction and tension, as the cycles start all over again.

It is easy to see how there are actually two cycles within a controlling relationship when you look at them side by side in this example.

Controlled Partner's Cycle	Controller's Cycle
Disillusionment, rising dissatisfaction	Growing tension
Determination to leave	Explosion
Growing fears, reassessment of the relationship, onset of denial, change of heart	Damage Control
Honeymoon	Honeymoon
Disillusionment, rising dissatisfaction	Growing tension

A control dynamic, like this one can be a lifelong dance, but it is a dance of misery for both partners. Each person fears losing the other person more than anything else.

Breaking free of these cycles requires overcoming an internal denial system that has been allowed to evolve over time. Again, it begins with poor self-esteem, which is the primary element in a relationship that evolves into one of control. A woman client once said that she was initially attracted to her husband because he was firm and did not let people tell him what to do. She saw this trait as a strength and believed she could always depend on him. It was not until much later that she realized that he wouldn't listen to her either. When asked to rate her level of self-esteem, she said she had no self-esteem.

Fears That Can Get in Your Way

It is important to face your fears, to understand and overcome them, if you really want to change your life. You can decide to end your relationship, or you can decide to try to end the controlling nature of the relationship. But you won't make much progress unless you deal with your fears of change.

Fear of the unknown develops over time as personal control and autonomy are surrendered to your partner. Along with giving up control and freedom comes a growing dependence on the controller. Another woman client was afraid to leave her home alone, afraid to go shopping without her husband, had never made a banking transaction without him, did not even carry cash on her. But thirty years before, when she was single, she had lived in her own apartment, worked to support herself, and had conducted a completely independent lifestyle. Over the length of the thirty-year marriage, she had simply forgotten that she had the skills to do anything she wanted, completely on her own.

There is also the fear of having to start all over in a new relationship, along with the twin fear of possibly never finding another person to love. People fear starting over only to end up in another controlling relationship.

There is also the fear of family rejection. There are many fears that combine to pressure people to remain in controlling relationships. It is only too easy to buy into the damage control of the controller, to create a self-deception that this time it will be different. One woman spoke of the great revelation her husband had experienced after she had threatened to leave him. He had supposedly "seen the light" and was truly going to change. She told her therapist that she had genuine hope that the relationship was finally going to become what she always had wanted it to be. But the truth was that this was her husband's seventh great revelation, and she was using the same words she had used on six prior occasions. Only by manipulating her own perceptions, by denying the reality that her husband's latest great revelation was actually nothing more than damage control, by manufacturing artificial hope within herself, was she able to talk herself out of doing what she feared most—leaving—and becoming free.

These examples are not given to send an overly negative message, but it is important to be clear that making the decision to free yourself from a controlling relationship requires a lot of courage. As wonderful as freedom is, it comes with a heavy price. The price is based on how long you allowed yourself to be imprisoned. Ultimately, your battle is with yourself—with your fears and insecurities. But if you believe in yourself and in your worth, the war can be won by either leaving the relationship altogether or by working with your partner to create something new that is not based on control.

There is nothing more valuable than personal freedom.

Exercise: Identifying Your Control Cycle

If you have been frustrated in your attempts to change or leave a controlling relationship, it may help to examine the dynamics that keep you hooked.

Compare your own experience with the cycles described earlier. Give it some thought and see if you can recognize similar stages of control in your own life. Is there a honeymoon period after a serious blow-up? Can you feel anger build in yourself and your partner? Do you tend to sense when there is another explosion just around the corner?

The two of you may have less clear-cut roles than in the above examples, and there may be different elements in your control cycle. One client described the period after an explosion as one in which the other person typically did not talk for several hours but would then start talking about anything under the sun except the problem or the explosion. In this case, a conspiracy had formed to deny the existence of the explosion and move on to the honeymoon stage.

It is important to see your own control behaviors clearly. Understanding how your own personal control cycle works is the first step in putting an end to it.

CHAPTER SIX

What to Do If You Decide to Stay

There are people who deliberately choose to remain in controlling relationships for a variety of reasons. The reasons may have to do with family, children, finances, religion, or other factors.

If you choose to stay in a controlling relationship is there a way to free your inner self? This is not an easy thing to do, but it is far from impossible. What you can make of the relationship depends a great deal on the attitude of your partner. However, even if your partner tries to maintain control, you have some options.

Becoming Free While Staying

It is not impossible to build a life alongside a marriage and conduct the search for fulfillment in that separate life. It is a difficult task, but it can be done. In this kind of life, freedom becomes the time spent on personal pursuits; in order to deal with the time spent within the controlling environment, you must develop the ability to endure. You have to adjust your definition of freedom accordingly so that it can include living in an atmosphere of control. You have to focus on the time you spend away from control. For example, freedom can mean deciding to spend three weeks with a brother in Florida and doing it; it can mean volunteering to spend a week at a youth camp as a counselor and doing it; but it cannot include moving into an apartment alone and making all the day-to-day life decisions without the input of the controller.

It would be a mistake to judge a person who chooses to remain within a controlling relationship. Being free includes the right to make life choices. There is no right or wrong here. It's a personal decision. The concern should be that life choices are made with awareness. Remaining within a controlling relationship threatens personal freedom and that freedom will have to be guarded vigilantly. A controller needs to destroy freedom in order to control. So if freedom is noticed, it will become the target of the controller. That is why the controlled person's time, friends, contact with outsiders, and so on are all gradually brought into the control system. Freedom is the natural antithesis of control.

There is a French song called "Anna" that is about Anne Frank, hiding from the Nazis in a Dutch attic. In the song, she heard the soldier's boots on the street below, but in her heart she kept a garden. She tried to focus on the garden and the flowers that bloomed there. Right through to the point when the soldiers took her away, she thought of the garden inside her heart. The song is beautiful, but it is also a vision of someone trying to remain free within a prison. You cannot share the secret garden with your controlling partner because your partner would try to destroy it.

For a person choosing to not leave a controlling relationship, perhaps the most common strategy is working to help the partner change and develop. There are cases where the partner actually does change. Unfortunately, those cases are rare. Most often, the partner is already traveling down his or her own personal life path, and control is so deep a part of that path, it is hard to let go. People arrive at their place in life through a process. Some are too invested in defenses to let go of them.

Controllers often see themselves as winners in the battle of the sexes, and do not believe that two people can be together without one person being a winner. All they see is the battle. It is hard to convince someone to put down a weapon when the weapon seems so essential. Remember, you can watch your partner evolve, but you can do very little to influence the evolution. It is not easy to teach someone else how to walk on your path. Still, you may feel you owe it to your partner and the relationship to try to change it into something free from control.

Regaining Trust Is Difficult

Many people are surprised at how difficult relationship issues can be to resolve. So many different things can make resolution difficult. Most often the biggest problem, on the inside of your own head and heart, is the question of lost trust. In the evolution of a controlling relationship, so many bad things can happen that trust is shattered and, for many, it can never be restored.

It is hard to let go of past hurts. There's a tendency to dwell on the bad things that happened in a relationship. They can be a source of ongoing argument and distress. However, to let go of the past, it is necessary to trust again. One reason you may keep dwelling on the bad things that happened is that you are afraid that bad things will happen again. It is natural to look for some kind of reassurance from your partner who was hurtful and controlling that, together, you will not slide back into the controlling pattern—and no such guarantee can be given. You either regain the trust you once had for your partner, or you do not. Trust is not earned, it is given. This time, unlike the first go-round, there is a bad track record to overcome before the trust can be given again.

This may be the hardest challenge for you to overcome, but it's not the only challenge. Here are some other questions: Can you regain respect for the person who controlled you for so long? Can you respect yourself after allowing yourself to be controlled? Can your partner respect you as an equal in a relationship after successfully pushing you down and controlling you? Can you become best buddies again? How about this one: Can you surrender mind, body, and spirit in the truest and most beautiful expression of physical love with the person who controlled you for so long? There are many difficult issues to overcome if the relationship is to be saved. When a relationship becomes one based on control, it is usually true that, over time, nothing in the relationship goes unaffected.

One more thought. The amount of effort you are willing to put into saving a relationship is dictated to some degree by your belief system. For some people, ending an unhappy relationship is the logical thing to do. For others, who may have married with the concept of spending an entire life with one person, ending the relationship seems wrong.

Whatever your beliefs, if you eventually decide to leave the relationship, you will find strength in knowing that you gave it your best shot. So you should ask yourself: Is there no other way? Is it not possible to be free within this relationship?

How Deciding to Stay Affects Your Partner

While many people may realize that the relationship they are in is a disaster, their partner may have no clue that anything is wrong. You could find yourself talking divorce and discover that your partner is totally astonished over the idea of ending the relationship. Has your partner initiated damage control or is this surprise real? Was your partner truly oblivious to the problems, to what has happened to the relationship, or is this reaction feigned as an attempt to gain time to work on you, to get you back?

There are no easy answers to these questions. However, people do have a natural tendency to avoid change. If you start talking about divorce, your partner will also have to deal with giving up what he or she knows and accepts. No matter how unhappy your partner may be, he or she also has an investment in the relationship and a natural hesitation about getting into unknown territory. So you can be fairly certain that your partner's initial reaction to your decision to end the relationship will be negative. Initially, your partner will probably focus on his or her losses and will probably see the potential changes as very negative.

Although you are approaching someone outside of yourself—your partner—the next step is still inside your own head. You have to deal with this question entirely on your own: "Shall I give the relationship another chance?" The difference at this precise moment, as opposed to all the other chances you may have given, is that you now have the issues out on the table and in the light, not hidden and ignored. This is an opportunity to talk things through, to sort out the issues, to clarify wants and needs, and to negotiate. Many people make this choice.

In talking with your partner, you may find that neither of you has ever defined your relationship, that both of you just took the relationship for granted, as a living entity, and never really examined it. Somewhere along the line, you discovered that you were being controlled, that you could not feel free in that environment, and that you wanted freedom more than anything else. Partners often say that they have never thought of themselves as controllers and do not want to control. Where do you go from here?

Setting Up the Relationship Negotiation

If you want to give the relationship another chance, the following steps are a practical way to go about it. This method is designed to help you organize the negotiation and guide your partner through the process of catching up to where you are now.

The first step is to share everything talked about so far with your partner. This is the time to use your analysis of your relationship (see chapter 4). You need to be very clear about what changes you want in your relationship. You must also give your partner time to work on his or her own analysis. After all, you have been moving toward this moment for a long time. Your partner may or may not have been equally dissatisfied with the relationship. This may all be new to your partner and it may take time to catch up. Compare your analysis with your partner's analysis. Are there areas of common ground? Areas that can be easily adjusted? For example, your partner may get angry when you are critical of minor things and you may get angry when your partner wants you to account for your time away from home. Perhaps a trade-off can be worked out and both of your can work on changing behaviors.

You both need to look at how each of your actions affects each other. You need to clearly understand how things must change behaviorally. But more important, you both need to grasp how attitudes and perceptions must change in order to avoid a relapse. The next section will describe this process in detail.

None of this is easy. You may even need an impartial outsider to help. Inside your own head, as you negotiate, you have to be comfortable with what is happening. Also, you have to be careful not to fool yourself; you have to watch for and avoid creating a new denial system.

Negotiation is very dangerous. You cannot really be sure that your partner's agreement to make changes is real until those changes are put into practice. But equally important, you cannot really be sure of your own thinking unless you are vigilant and honest with yourself. With the two assessments shared between you, you are ready to move to the next stage.

The Process of Negotiation

Can the negotiation work? Sometimes it does. You can maximize the chance of it working by taking several steps. Remember that it is important to negotiate without anger. That may sound impossible, but it is necessary. Negotiation is supposed to be a constructive thing and anger is a destructive force. If partners have angry things to say to each other, it needs to be done outside of the negotiation process. This can actually be done. You can set aside specific times to discuss past hurts when you are not negotiating. The best thing you can do during these times is to listen to your partner. Yes, you have all those things inside that need to come out, but do it in a balanced way. It is important to learn how your partner sees things. This will help you to understand your role in the awful dance you were doing together. You were there, remember? You did participate. The controlling relationship did not come about in a vacuum. It is very important to understand how you react to control, so you can avoid it in the future, whether with your current partner or someone else.

In addition to negotiating without anger, it is also important to negotiate without judgment. Not judging each other can be just as difficult as not getting angry. You have to agree to suspend such ideas as who's to blame, who was right or wrong, during the negotiation. You begin with the idea that you did not walk down the aisle conspiring together to make each other as miserable as possible for as many years as possible. You do not get up each morning trying to figure how best to screw up the other person during the course of the coming day. You have to assume, and hope that the assumption is valid, that the hurtful things you do to each other are not deliberate. Well, to be more realistic, you should assume that hurtful actions did not start as deliberate actions designed to hurt each other. With that as a starting point, the negotiation can take on a constructive character rather than an accusing combative one.

In a negotiation, you may also get a chance to learn some things about your partner's character. Remember, knowledge is power. The more knowledge you can gather, the better you can make decisions. As you learn what brought your partner to do hurtful, unloving things, you can learn more about your partner. Throughout the negotiation, you should always be asking the question: Will this work? The more you learn about how your partner thinks and perceives things, especially how your partner perceives you and relationships in general, the better you will be able to answer that question.

So the negotiation should be mutual, and free from blame and accusation. The relationship evolved as a process. Now the two of you are examining that process and trying to work out ways to improve it. The more you can see the process, rather than the specific things that happened, the more objective you can be and, in turn, the more your chances of succeeding will increase. You see, in a real negotiation, you and your partner have actually become partners again—or perhaps for the first time. You have developed a common goal and must work together, as a team, to achieve that goal.

Give Yourself Time

It is important to allow plenty of time for this to work. The analysis each of you completed gives you specific things to change. You should try to focus on plans of action that accommodate your differences. For example, it is not helpful to make this kind of suggestion: "Be more patient while we are shopping." It is much better to have this as a change: "When we are shopping and you start to get impatient, let me know. If I am finished, we can go, but if I need more time, you can go off on your own and we will meet at the car at a specified time." It's impossible to fake patience, but you can have an alternative action plan for when impatience happens—a behavior that is acceptable to both persons. What you really want to stop, when impatience happens, is your partner's frowning face, heavy sighs, and mournful looks that are designed to make you feel guilty, which is controlling behavior.

New habits take time to develop. People, being imperfect, make mistakes. Change does not come overnight. Both of you need to change. You each need a mechanism to stop the control game in its tracks. The controller needs to be shown his or her control techniques. The controlled person needs to be shown his or her games that lead to control. Partners can do these things for each other (rather than to each other).

It is also possible to be conned by a partner who is not really invested in change. You will eventually find out when your partner resorts to the old behaviors. If you think this is happening, you may call your partner on it and get a denial back. "I was not doing that. You just misunderstood me." Bad sign! Someone really invested in change would want to understand your perception: "I did not mean to send that message; what made you think I was trying to control you? Let's talk about it."

Someone truly wanting to change is someone wanting to talk things out, wanting to understand, wanting to avoid a relapse. Both of you need to agree to put more energy into working on the relationship. It's a bad sign if you find your partner coming up with supposedly more important things to do. In therapy, couples often say that they just did not have time to get to their real issues. Yet there is nothing more important than improving your life, of which your life together is an essential part. How can something else get in the way?

Be vigilant about not falling into your old habits. When your partner does one thing, you have developed a habitual response. This response could initiate the awful dance all over again. The longer the relationship has lasted, the greater the danger of you giving in to the same old set of controls. Giving in becomes even harder to resist if controlling relationships are all you have ever known. Buying into the denial system will seem like the natural thing to do. So watching yourself during this process is extremely important.

If the negotiation is going to work, you will soon know. You will see change, real change—in both of you. Also, you should find your self-esteem, and that of your partner, going up. You should be feeling better about yourself rather than worse. The two of you should start feeling like mutual winners. You should also notice that each of you are focused on the other and the needs of the other.

So, if the negotiation is going to work, you will know it. Again, if it is not working, you may not know as easily. Here are some further clues: If the changes in the relationship are not real, you will find no spontaneous jumps forward, no improved feeling about yourself, no boost in the self-esteem department, and certainly no sense of winning together. Instead, the sense of competition will still be there, lurking just under the surface.

Remember, your decisions are under your control at all times. You may decide you have made a decision that becomes unacceptable. You get to change your mind. If you reach a point where you decide that staying in the relationship is no longer acceptable, you can rethink your position and choose the other option, to leave the relationship. This is not a sign of failure, it is being realistic. Failure is freezing yourself into a position that is not acceptable and not allowing yourself to move forward.

CHAPTER SEVEN

What to Do If You Decide to Leave

Once you have decided to leave a controlling relationship, you may find it is not so simple. Many people have come to a moment of decision—the moment of facing the fact that their only true option is to end things—and many of them have still chosen to remain in their relationships.

When you look at the situation objectively, it can be difficult to understand why they would. It would seem almost a given that you would not hesitate to make a self-supporting and self-enhancing decision, actually a survival decision, to get away from control, and try to live on your own. However, if you are in a controlling relationship and have tried but found it impossible to leave, you can be certain that you are not alone. The reasons why it is so hard to leave must be explored if you are to get past them.

It has already been said that many people have been able to avoid control in their relationships. Many others have been able to see it as it began to occur, and put an end to it. Many have been able to work with partners to develop accommodation rather than competition and control struggles. So what makes it so hard for some people to leave controlling relationships behind?

Overcoming the Enemy Called Fear

People will say that they have put five years, or ten years or twenty years, of their lives into a relationship and that they cannot just walk away from such a long-term investment. One woman actually said: "He took away my youth." Statements of this kind are almost always accompanied by fears that lie just below the anger and indignation.

Imagine an old-fashioned balancing scale. On one side of the scale is the Known. On the other side of the scale is what may be called the Big Question Mark. The Known is life as you live it, your day-to-day existence, and your relationships, especially your relationships. You have a marriage, a life partner, and a marital existence. In this example, what matters is the kind of relationship you have, the way you interact together, the way you communicate and live together. All this is known to you. To give it up, you have to enter the world of the Big Question Mark.

No matter how unhappy you may be, your relationship is familiar territory and you know how to survive in it. You have learned to cope and, at some level, to meet needs. At least you can meet enough of your needs to make life tolerable. But you know nothing about what life would be like outside of this relationship. You have no idea what will happen next if you opt for the Big Question Mark over what is Known. That is frightening. It is only natural that the longer a person is in a relationship, the more frightening the Big Question Mark becomes. For most people who leave relationships, what they know must actually be worse than anything the future might hold.

You can use the same balancing scale to measure other things. For example, on one side you can have all the unhappiness of a relationship. On the other side, you can place all the good things: children, financial security, material things, acceptance of family and friends, those freedoms you may have developed alongside the relationship, even the good times you had with your partner. There are many positives in any relationship, even a controlling relationship.

As long as you are not actively thinking about ending a relationship, it is somehow easy to look at and dwell on the negatives. However, as soon as you begin to seriously look at ending a relationship, for some reason you may begin to notice the positives. This is a common tendency. It is as though people change from focusing on what they put up with to what they will be giving up. To leave the relationship, your imaginary scale has to show that the negatives far outweigh the positives.

Fear the Worst

If you leave an unhealthy relationship, what is the very worst thing that can happen? What is the thing you fear the most? Depending on who you are, your answer will differ. "The worst" is not the same for everyone. For some people, it is the prospect of starting over with a new relationship. They may fear that they will never trust another person again. Some people will say they do not know if they can ever trust their own judgment again. This is especially true for people who have been in unhealthy relationships for a long time; the thought of going all the way back to the beginning, of starting all over with someone else, is nearly unthinkable.

For most people, the worst thing that can happen is not finding someone else. The fear of being alone, of growing old alone, seems like the worst thing that can happen. A lot of people get invloved with someone new before they choose to leave their marriage. This is one solution, but most of these new relationships end up to be carbon copies of the ones they leave. This is because they do not allow themselves a chance to heal after getting out of their controlling relationships. You need a period of time to sort things out, to understand how the control happened, how the control got into what seemed to be a relationship with great potential—and how to avoid letting it happen again.

Fear of Starting Over

For many people, however, it is not the next relationship that is the source of their fear. They are simply worried about having to start all over. Everything they had and did was tied up with their partners. Suddenly everything is on their shoulders alone. There is no partner to help. Granted, the amount of help that was available when the relationship was intact varies and, in some cases, may have been nonexistent. But there may still be a sense of not having been in this thing we call life totally alone. "No matter how manipulating, demanding, unsupportive my partner was, at least I had a partner." Being alone can be very lonely. Think of a working mom, with a household that includes a number of children, all with issues of their own, suddenly facing the prospect of having her partner move out and being left with all the responsibilities and, probably, a greatly reduced income. This is a scary future to face.

Changing on the Inside

These impediments to breaking free have a common denominator. They are all determined by what people think or believe will happen. It is extremely rare for people to remain in relationships because they are forced to do so by outside influences. Granted, sometimes there may be threats. "If I leave, he said he would kill himself and I cannot handle that guilt." But it is also rare that threats of violence are seriously meant. Yes, there are stalkers out there. There are people out there who do horrible things to the people who try to leave them, but they are rare. Those who would actually commit an act of violence will probably have been violent before. For most people who wrestle with the question of staying or leaving a controlling relationship, the struggle is happening inside their own heads. It is a personal issue.

Change has to begin on the inside. If you really are going to leave a controlling relationship, the first thing you have to change is the perception that the relationship is normal. The myth of normalcy has to be shattered before any movement can occur. You must recognize that there is something wrong, that you deserve better, that unhappiness and being unfulfilled are not inevitable. You must fight self-doubt and accept that facing your fears is necessary if you want to be free. The good news is that you can be incredibly flexible if you want to be. You truly are capable of changing how you look at life and how you define such things as normal, at virtually any stage of life.

Outside Influences

If you find you must leave, what next? It may be—in fact it is often the case—that your partner does not want to end the relationship. You will find yourself pressing onward alone, maybe with direct opposition. You must prepare.

It is also true that family and friends—your support system—may serve as obstacles to change. You may have assumed they would be helpful, but they might not be.

Change almost always carries a price—and the longer you've been stuck in one pattern, the heavier the price of changing. For example, if you are married twenty-five years, have four children (with their four spouses) and eight grandchildren, and want to divorce your controlling spouse and free yourself, you have seventeen other people to consider. Your decision is going to, in some way, affect all of them. If you are eighteen, single, and breaking off an abusive relationship, there are very few other people involved in your decision. You may even find you have a cheering section of friends and family giving you standing ovations as you move through the process.

If you've been married a long time, you will probably have a group of immediate family members frantically trying to decide who should have the next holiday dinner that was traditionally at your home, which parent they should invite, and what they will have to do to appease the one that was not invited. This may not seem very serious at first glance but take this one example and multiply it by every social occasion that typically involves you and your spouse. Every one of those occasions will be altered if the relationship ends.

It is easy to see why so often family members and even close friends may develop an investment in keeping you inside the controlling relationship, even if they are all fully aware of how unhappy you are while in it. It is not that they wish you unhappiness, it is just that the changing of an established pattern is always upsetting to those around the edges of the pattern. You need to look at this in more detail because it really can turn out to be a major impediment to ending a relationship.

Change of Status

When you married, the perception of who you are changed in the eyes of your extended family and friends. The perception of who your partner is also changed in the eyes of his or her extended family and friends. It was no longer "Bill" and it was no longer "Emily." There was suddenly a new entity known as "Emily-and-Bill." There was also a sudden expansion of friends and relatives as the two of you begin to share your individual circles with one another. You both invited your friends to parties and you invited both of your families to family functions.

Look at the relationship through the eyes of the children of this entity called "Emily-and-Bill," as they watch their parents move toward ending their relationship. If the children are young, there will probably be pressure from them to keep the controlling relationship intact because they believe they are totally dependent on both parents being together. If they are older but still living in the home, their definition of home life usually includes both parents. This is where the process of defining normal can come back to haunt you. Children are often resistant to having that definition changed, no matter how unhappy they themselves may be in, what is to them, their normal home environment. If they are grown, out on their own, married and have children of their own, then they are less dependent. But then there are even more people invested in "Emily-and-Bill."

A man in his forties once said, "Oh, my God! If this divorce of my parents really goes through, my mother could actually start having sex with other men!" The thought was terrifying because he would have to think of his mother in a whole new way. For him, the unhappily married and often complaining mom was a lot easier to accept.

The Challenge to Friendships

In addition to this pressure to keep things "normal" and not make waves through the interconnected circles of families and friends, there may be another factor at work. Some friends and relatives may develop a quite natural but very serious caution about supporting this major change—your ending the controlling relationship—based on the fear that you will not go through with it. This is more likely to be true if you have made attempts at other times, only to falter. After a while, you are like the boy who cried wolf, and the cheering section gets smaller with each failed attempt. Those who remain become quieter and quieter in their encouragements. After all, they feel foolish when they have to listen to the reasons for canceling the big move over and over again.

This kind of indecision can eventually hurt your friendships. Think of it from this way: You decide to leave your partner of so many years, and a friend of yours becomes the head of your cheering section. What happens to that friend if you change your mind? Your partner will definitely see your friend as a threat. You, in your commitment to saving the relationship, may even feel the same way about your friend, who knows the whole story and all the factors leading to your decision to leave. You may even find that you have a hard time facing and dealing with your friend. This last will be especially true when you know deep inside that the relationship will not work. Such friendships have a hard time surviving a reconciliation.

With all this in mind, it may become easier to understand why friends and extended family will often view taking any position, other than that of neutrality, as a no-win position for them. They may see it as dangerous to voice any opinion once you tell them you have made the decision to leave your partner. To be honest, ending a committed relationship is not easy, and many people are ultimately not able to go through with it, so you cannot blame people for taking what they see as a safe and cautious position (which is actually taking no position at all).

Who's on Your Side

Finally, family and friends tend to think of troubled relationships as having a good guy and a bad guy. However, as the relationship begins to physically come apart, as lines in the sand become more clearly drawn, as, perhaps, bad feelings enter into the breaking up process and tempers become strained, loyalties tend to divide along bloodlines. That is to say, no matter who is the original "problem" in a relationship, in the end, Emily's family will side with her, and Bill's family will side with him. Typically, old friends end up siding with the partner who was their friend before the relationship first formed.

The sudden lack of outside support may be the biggest surprise you will experience when you make the decision to leave a controlling relationship. You may find yourself feeling all alone. Indeed sympathy may initially shift to the person left behind. You may feel a tremendous sense of abandonment and betrayal if you don't keep a good perspective. You have to understand that everyone has an agenda, no matter how close he or she seems to you.

The truth is you must prepare to make this struggle alone. You cannot count on support. While it is true that you will find some support from the outside, it is dangerous to count on it before you begin the process. It is even more dangerous to count on specific people to stand by you; there are too many unknown factors involved. In other words, it's a good idea to plan for the worst and hope for the best.

Open Opposition

As noted, you may encounter open opposition from your partner. You already know the techniques your partner will use in the attempt to stop your move toward freedom. You can be certain your partner will try all the techniques that have worked on you in the past. There will be variations, of course. There are always variations. You can also expect increases in intensity with the passage of time. Damage control will become more dramatic, the promises will become more enticing, tears will flow more freely, confessions of love will be more emotional, self-chastising will become more frequent, and so on. There will be more sugar and it will taste sweeter. Be aware of your control cycles. Awareness will help you resist old habits.

During open opposition, your partner will try to touch any emotion that might weaken you or bring you to reconsider your decision. The primary emotions that will be targeted are guilt and fear. This is because they are the most responsive to control. But they are not the only emotions a controller can go after. In direct opposition, there are no rules and there is no such thing as fair.

The problem is that there is very little you can do to combat open opposition short of taking legal steps. Yet in most situations, legal steps can only be taken after you file for divorce. It is really hard to deal with open opposition when the controller is still living in the home with you.

There is really only one response to open opposition. Do not play the game. Do not engage in the conversations, the entreaties, the attempts to get you to believe the problems are really your fault, the attempts to negotiate away the problems, the threats or any other gambits that may be thrown your way. Remember, in this scenario, you have already tried negotiation or rejected it as unworkable. It is like your vocabulary has been reduced to just a few words and phrases: "No! Stop! I won't discuss it! I know what you are doing! This will not work!" Stay with the process.

The simpler you keep things, the better you will get through open opposition. A controller this desperate cares nothing about logic or right and wrong. A controller cares only about how to get what he or she wants. Remember the concept of the mental toolshed. As long as you stay in a simple, black-and-white world, you can avoid the games. Remember, mind games are not like solitaire; it takes two to play a mind game. If you do not participate, it cannot work.

Coercion As a Form of Open Opposition

Open opposition can even take the form of coercion. Your partner may try to force you to change your decision. This can take the form of threats, stalking behaviors, spying, and, in extreme cases, violence. If the controller gets frustrated, it will become harder to predict how far he or she might go to stop you from leaving.

Frustration can surface in a number of ways, but typically it surfaces as anger. How anger is expressed depends on the character of the angry person. What do you do if your partner becomes violent? What if you are threatened? What if you are hit? What if those in your support system are threatened? What if the controller threatens self-injury? What if the controller acts on that threat?

The first thing to understand is that the situation could get serious. Regardless of how much you may believe that nothing bad is going to happen, it is important to treat it as though something bad will happen. If you are going to make a mistake, you want to err on the side of caution. You also want to send out the message that you are not going to tolerate unacceptable behavior. If you are threatened or if violence occurs, you must get in touch with the appropriate authorities right away. You may go to the police or to a domestic violence shelter, where you can stay while you sort out things. If you feel threatened, you must take action. If you accept the unacceptable behavior, there is no protection out there for you.

Again, violence is rare in cases where partners have never been violent in the past. Most cases don't come to this. Generally, you can get through open opposition by not participating. In most cases, simply naming the game will end the game.

The End of Open Opposition

How do you know you have come through open opposition and that this phase of breaking away is really over? You can usually tell by your partner's behavior. There are a couple of typical scenarios. Your spouse may develop the attitude that you were not good enough for him or her in the first place. This attitude is actually very good for you. It is a signal that your partner has found a face-saving way to move on. By developing an attitude of superiority, your partner no longer faces the concept of being the loser at the end of the relationship. The more your partner looks down on you, the more certain you can be that open opposition is truly over.

A second reaction is a dramatic change in character. Your partner may suddenly turn to religion or suddenly discover the potentials of returning to the single life. These are two common reactions, but there are other possibilities.

It is still necessary to be careful. Your partner's religious rebirth could carry the message, "How can you doubt that I have really changed? Can't you see that I have finally found God?" The rediscovery of the joys of the single life could carry the message, "Don't be so hasty. I may find someone else. If you suddenly come to your senses and want to come back, I may be already involved with another." Don't be fooled.

Ending a Relationship and the Children

There can be a lot of guilt associated with breaking up a family if the breakup involves children, particularly dependent minor children. It's generally believed that two-parent families are better for children than single parent households. The assumption is the two-parent household is a healthier environment. But what if the environment is not healthy? Remember that, more than anything else, parents teach their children and model what their children will come to define as normal. So you have to ask the question, do you want to teach your children to define unhappy as the normal state of a committed relationship?

It is easy to buy into a guilt trip when thinking about the well-being of your children. It takes a lot to look beyond the immediate situation and see the bigger picture. You have to keep a certain discipline by looking at what is really best in the long run.

As was already discussed, the children themselves will probably have an investment in keeping the marriage together. Remember, this family existence is all they know, and the prospect of change may scare them. They have already adjusted to trouble areas that directly affect them, and it is only natural for them to fight such a fundamental change to their existence. This can increase a sense of guilt in the mind of the person breaking away. That is why there is a real need to keep focusing on the big picture, and of what is really best for all concerned. Do you want to teach your children that they should become sacrificial animals for the rest of their lives, or do you want to teach them that, when they make a mistake, they should correct it?

There is another issue involving the children. If you are the one wanting to end the relationship and your partner wants to keep it going, your partner may try to set you up as the bad guy, and try to enlist the children as allies in the fight to save the family. This is very difficult to fight. How do you explain to your children that, although you are ending the family structure as it currently exists, you are not the bad guy and you are not abandoning them? There are two key issues on which to focus: first, that your love for your children has not decreased in any way. In fact, their well-being is likely part of your decision to end the marriage. The other key point is that you are not ending the family so much as restructuring it in a more healthy way. There will still be a family. The children will still have two parents and have access to both of them. It is just that the adults are being separated because they are not functioning well together. The children may not understand this at first, but, as they get settled into the new structure, they will hopefully see that they have not lost their parents. What they have lost is that tense and stressful environment that existed when their parents were together.

Turning children into pawns in a struggle between adults is particularly evil. No one should be allowed to get away with that kind of manipulation. Unfortunately, it happens all too often. Your best defense, if you find it happening to you and your children, is to not engage in it. It is important to understand that this kind of manipulation is most successful with younger children. Most adolescents have figured out what is really going on between their parents and are not so easily fooled.

Manipulators should know that one day their behavior will come back to haunt them. Children grow up. When they reach the age where abstract reasoning kicks in, they are going to figure out what was done to them, and when they do, they are going to be angry.

If you are on the receiving end of the manipulation, hang in there. Even if your children seem to be set against you while they are being manipulated, when they figure out what is being done to them, they will come back to you. That is why it is so important to avoid joining manipulation games. You can be honest and you can defend yourself, but you do not want to be lumped together with the manipulator when your children's anger kicks in. Keep to the high ground.

Preparing to Break Free

So, there are many hurdles, most of which are predictable. Do your homework, get the information you need, gain the knowledge necessary to break away with as little trouble and as little loss as possible. If you are in a marriage, it will probably mean divorce. There are a number of lawyers who offer an initial consultation at no cost. Take advantage of that service. You can quickly learn what to expect in a divorce or dissolution; you can learn about custody issues, the local rules on child support, potential for alimony, how property is usually distributed, whether you can keep medical insurance coverage, and so on. Such a consultation, whether there is a charge or not, can take a lot of the mystery and, perhaps, a lot of the anxiety out of the next steps.

The next thing you do is develop a plan. You may need to find a place to live. You could stay with a friend or a relative, but only for a short period of time. It is usually best not to plan on staying at someone else's place for very long. If you are leaving your partner, filing for divorce, working through open opposition, and all the other complicating factors that can be involved with breaking free, you are carrying a tremendous amount of stress baggage. The disruption to another home, family, and lifestyle cannot really be estimated ahead of time, and you don't want to put a strain on your relationships with friends or relatives. So, no matter how accommodating friends or relatives may seem, it is best to keep your stay brief.

If you are planning to leave a relationship by moving out of your home, plan far enough ahead so that you can save enough money to pay at least two months worth of rent and utilities in a reasonable apartment, along with the cost of food and other necessities. The security deposit on most apartments usually matches a month's rent. You should have a safety net of a full month.

If there are children involved and you want them with you, it is usually better to file for divorce right away, and include temporary custody and the right to remain in the family home as part of the petition. When the breakdown of a relationship has reached this point, it is best to think practically and not sentimentally. One of the biggest mistakes people can make at this stage of breaking free is to feel guilty and responsible, to want everything to be "fair." The other person is most likely very angry and looking for any way they can find to hurt you and get back at you. You need to keep a level head. Think practically, and think in terms of the future. You are going to have to survive and get on with your life.

That First Bad Night

There is another thing to prepare for ahead of time—the first bad night. The actual first night may be one of relief and exhilaration. However, the first bad night will come along; you can be sure of that. It is the night when you are lying in bed and you suddenly find yourself struggling with all the doubts in the world. All the things that could go wrong suddenly dominate your thoughts. Some of the things and plans you may have taken for granted may be backfiring on you. There will be unforeseen problems. You cannot think of everything ahead of time or prepare for every contingency. You may become very frightened and unsure of yourself. You may question all the decisions you made and all the assumptions on which your decisions were based. At a time like this, everything comes into question.

It is important to know that the first bad night is normal. It would be abnormal not to go through it to some degree. You have, after all, opted for the Big Question Mark. Why would you not go through a period of terrible doubt? The second thoughts you may have about the wisdom of leaving are often anchored in the knowledge that you were able to survive in the controlling relationship, that it was at least known territory.

This is a time when your faith in yourself will be tested. Many have gotten this far, actually have left the controller, only to falter when this final self-doubt sets in. You could become your own worst enemy. You could relapse, negate the insights you gained on your journey away from the controlling relationship, and cancel the conclusions you reached about what you need in order to live a free life. You could listen to others who have their own agendas and take on their ideas as though they were meant only for your well-being. This is the time when you can feel your loneliest, your most abandoned, and the most unsure of yourself. You may question your inner voice even though that inner voice is the very spirit you are trying to set free. This is the time for faith in yourself, it is the only thing that will see you through.

This time of self-doubt is a time of trial. It is a time when you may feel a need for another person in your life. But you have to know with certainty that you can make it on your own—relying only on your resources, to be successfully independent without help from anyone—before you can be certain that you are ready for another relationship. In fact, it is the only way you can be in a relationship and remain free. Anything less can lead to another control situation. Self-doubt is only natural at this moment; it's what you do with it that matters.

The first bad night has a purpose. It marks the beginning of your test to prove that you can really make it on your own. Everyone should have a chance to live as an independent adult. A lot of people go from living with their parents directly into marriage and, as a result, never learn how much survival ability they actually have. The world outside of their safe haven appears somewhat mysterious and frightening. People who move out on their own and live a few years as independent adults learn how easy life can be if they make a few basic logical choices and exercise a fair amount of self-discipline. These people are ultimately much less dependent on their partners and, therefore, less willing to be controlled.

If you are out there on your own for the first time, or if it has been a long time since you have been on your own, or if your circumstances have changed dramatically since you were last on your own, then words of encouragement are not going to help very much. You still have to go through it. You have to look objectively at finances, for example. You have to look at the whole survival picture. You have to develop a list of things that absolutely, positively, need to be done, and you have to prioritize the items on that list. You will need a schedule, a daily routine that will help you get all the things done that need doing.

You will also have to fight the frozen feeling that can grow inside of you and push aside your self-doubt. You will have to become active. After all, you are in a war with yourself as the target, and you are the only one who can defend you. If there are children with you, you will have to take their fears and insecurities into consideration. You will need to appear strong and confident for them. There is a very practical struggle ahead of you, and everything inside of you may be screaming for nothing but the chance to shut down all operations. Life can only get better as long as you don't surrender.

Who Leaves Whom

You may think there are more controlling men out there than controlling women, but this is not the case. There are as many men being controlled in relationships as there are women. In fact, men are most likely the ones to be striking out on their own, moving into strange apartments, having to buy the essentials for independent living, and so on. In many cases, there are children involved in a breakup and, most often, the mothers have temporary custody and remain in the family home. So the majority of those starting new are more likely to be men than women. Men who break away from controlling relationships may have a harder time than women in their position. They may be more paralyzed by the first bad night. Let's face it, in most families, the nuts and bolts of the day-to-day operation are organized and run by women. It is usually women who plan meals, do the grocery shopping, and have a general routine going. This means it can be more difficult for men to get organized in the basic process of living independently. This breaking free process is not easy for anyone.

If the first bad night is the bottom of the pit, how deep will your particular pit be? It will be less deep if you have a job that brings in enough income to support yourself and, if they are with you, your children. If you are not earning a living, you may be able to file for temporary child (or spousal) support to keep going until you are legally divorced. You may have to rely on parents for temporary support. In the worst case, you may have to investigate public assistance in the form of housing, food stamps, and job search or training programs. The help is out there, but you have to find it. It is time for you to begin taking control of your life.

Who Is There for You

The time comes when you need to find out who, among your friends and family, has abandoned you and who is going to be there for you. Once you have identified your allies, you have to figure out how they can best help you. The big secret in dealing with supporters is to depend on them as little as possible but not be afraid to ask for help when you need it in specific areas. If you need to check out public assistance, for example, maybe a friend can watch the children while you do the footwork. Someone else may supply an emergency place to stay for a night, but the next morning it is up to you to look for a longer term housing solution.

As you begin to establish your independence, it's important not to lean too heavily on others. Clearly you don't want to wear out your welcome. But, more importantly, you really need to begin to create inside yourself the feeling that you are running your own ship from here on out. You need to know that you are in charge. You need some initial successes to give you the confidence to keep going. That will not happen if you rely too much on others to do things for you.

Here is something to remember. The world out there is less cold and cruel than it is merely impersonal. Most people don't care what happens to you. Most people are so lost in their own lives that they are not paying attention to what you are doing. This may seem frightening, but it is really a positive thing. If no one is watching to see if you mess up or not, then you are basically free to do what you want with your life. There is freedom in an impersonal world.

You are not being overwhelmed with bad luck. You are not in a hostile environment. There is no fate trying to drag you back to your controller. Mostly, the environment is a neutral one. Mostly, you make your own luck. Much of what is called luck is actually a product of how well you plan things. Yes, there are exceptions. There will be that late train that held you up just long enough for you to miss out on that perfect and reasonably priced apartment you wanted so badly. It is up to you how you interpret such an event. The truth is that you do not have an enemy out there trying to sabotage you, other than your ex-controller, even though you may feel that way when times are tough.

To be realistic, it is possible that your former controller also has allies invested in getting you back into the relationship. Those allies may even be people you thought would be your allies when you started the break. There may be very well-meaning people out there who might try to sabotage your efforts to gain freedom, and they may do it, convinced that they are acting in your best interest.

Your biggest threat may be what goes on inside you. If you are in a panic state, if you are confused and unclear about what to do to establish yourself, you may have trouble. If you are focused on your loneliness rather than your freedom, you may be setting yourself up for a relapse. Remember the cycles of the controller and the controlled. If you doubt yourself, if the Known becomes more attractive than the Big Question Mark, you could give the controller the signal to shift back into damage control. There will be times when rejoining that old cycle may appear to be the more attractive option.

Taking Action Helps

This is your vulnerable time and you must fight it with action. Finding a place to stay, securing an income, creating a budget, formulating a long-term plan, getting legal help: these actions will help you gain the confidence that you can handle life without control. Life is really not so impossible once you break it down to its main components. There are certain things you need to make it in our society, and there are ways of obtaining those things. But there are steps you need to take.

It is not really the act of leaving the controlling relationship that frees you. Freeing yourself is a state of mind. It is having the certain knowledge that you do not need the oversight or guidance of another to make it in this world. It is knowing that you have a place in life that is entirely yours. It is knowing that you can belong but not be owned, that you want to participate but not be ordered or directed, that you can live by your own rules as long as they do not infringe on another person's life and rules. It is knowing that you have your own unique niche in the scheme of things and that your destiny is yours to command.

The price of this kind of freedom may be extremely high. The price depends on where you are coming from and what you have to do to get where you want to go. The price of freedom varies from person to person, from circumstance to circumstance. The only common factor is the glory of freedom once it is achieved. For each person who sets out on this journey, there will be a different situation to overcome. There will be different challenges. The level of struggle and the intensity of opposition will vary. But the goal is the same. You have a sacred duty to free yourself. It is the only way you can truly exist and advance. It is the only way you can live as a truly integrated person.

Exercise: Preparing for Your Freedom

This chapter has focused on a number of things you will need to do if you leave a relationship. Depending on how long you were in the relationship and how dependent you may have become on your partner, leaving may be difficult or relatively easy. Either way, it is best to plan ahead. This exercise is designed to help you organize the process if you are preparing to leave. It should help you develop a logical and comprehensive plan of action.

In your notebook, list the following on separate pages: Support System, Housing, Income, Budget, Transportation, Child Care. Next, go back and try to plan how you will deal with each one.

The support system category may seem strange, but it may be the most important. The people who will support you can help you through many things, such as open opposition and the bad nights. True, there may be surprises in store. Not everyone on your list will necessarily be on your side, but try to think it through as well as you can. List friends and relatives first, then cross off those who are not likely to help. Do not forget the public agencies that may be helpful. Some human services offices provide day care, for example.

Do your homework on housing. Where will you live initially? What can you afford on your own? How will you find an apartment? How much will you need to start, and how long will it take you to save the money?

Work through each of the categories. Then go into action. Watch the classifieds, go look at some apartments, learn about start-up costs for utilities, base a budget on what you learn. Plan how you will get around and who will care for your children when you are working. You will find yourself getting good at preparation. This will make you less afraid and unsure of yourself.

Often people make decisions and then act on them immediately. This can be a mistake. It is usually best, especially when making major, life-changing decisions, to develop a plan before acting on a decision. The other purpose of this exercise is to slow you down, prepare you, and minimize the pain of the transition.

CHAPTER EIGHT

How to Connect and Still Remain Free

If you are in a controlling relationship, or have recently escaped one, you may wonder if it's truly possible to be in a relationship that is not based on control. You may ask yourself: "Can I really be in a committed relationship and still be free?" It is clear how easily controlling relationships happen, even for people who do not want them.

Most people want to be free. Most people don't want to be in controlling relationships. But there is another truth about nearly everyone. Most people want to feel connected. There is something inside of us, something deeply ingrained, that makes us want to bond. It is not logical and it is not physical. You could say this need is spiritual. The spirit wants to be free and to be connected at the same time.

Before you can connect with another person and form a healthy relationship, you have a little homework to do. So far, you've learned about change beginning on the inside and about taking yourself back. Basically, that was about healing from the loss of self-esteem and getting rid of the belief in your inadequacy. However, if you are coming out of a controlling relationship, that is only the first step.

You still have a set of relationship habits you developed while in a controlling relationship. If you do not break these habits, they could resurface when you begin to relate to a new person.

Breaking Old Habits

You will not be ready for another relationship until you heal from the controlling relationship you were in. This is important if you are going to avoid starting a relationship that will evolve into a mirror image of the one that you just ended. You have to undo the habits you formed as you participated in the development of control. There is a real danger that you could, by continuing old behavior patterns, start a new controlling process. You also have to be able to avoid any temptation to move toward becoming a controller (before your new partner has a chance to control you). You have to get completely over the previous relationship, and the things it did to you—and the things you did to you—before you can walk cleanly into a new relationship.

This may not be easy and it may take some time to accomplish. You need to examine the bad things that happened during the controlling relationship. You need to look at the things you did to yourself in order to survive with control. What personal compromises did you make? In what ways did you sell out to placate your partner? Remember, compromising yourself means giving away a part of yourself. It is necessary to make yourself whole again before getting into another relationship. You need to feel confident about your ability to be in a relationship that is free from control. If you are afraid of compromising yourself, you will only bring uncertainty into your next relationship and do further damage to your self-esteem.

Self-compromise can cause more harm than any outside abuse or control. It is like having one part of yourself betray another part. Much of your personal journey has to do with learning to defend yourself and not compromise. But another part of the journey, if you are to be truly healthy, is to accept that you are not perfect, and that you may have made some bad choices.

Compromise vs. Self-Compromise

In the beginning, you trusted yourself. Life was seemingly simple. You began with a very concrete, black-and-white view of life and it is only with time that you discerned shades of gray. With this loss of innocence came compromises.

There is no way around it, to exist in a world filled with other living beings, compromises are a necessary part of life. People make these compromises to co-exist as comfortably as possible. You drive on the right side of the road in order to co-exist peacefully with all the other drivers on the road. Such a compromise is good for everyone. It is a compromise designed to create order out of potential chaos. The alternative, after all, is to demand your right to drive anywhere on the road that you wish.

But when you compromise your spirit, you are doing more than co-existing, you are affecting your inner existence. It would be like giving up your right to drive at all so that everyone else can get where they need to go. Deeper yet is the compromise to live in an environment that enslaves the spirit. To choose to live in an environment that is demeaning, to choose to do things that you are against in order to avoid a clash with another, to choose to surrender things that are important—these are compromises of the spirit.

When you make these kinds of compromises, something changes inside. You don't lose your spirit, but you do lose faith in yourself.

To enter a new relationship and avoid falling back into old patterns, that trust, that inner sense of security, has to be reestablished. You may have gained one piece of wisdom which is that, since it happened once, it could happen again. But you also, hopefully, gained the awareness to stop it from happening again.

A woman named Jane had been in several physically abusive relationships. She is now in a relationship with a very gentle person. He is a person who, quite simply, is not capable of being abusive to a woman. This is a great step for her, but instead of settling into the relationship, she is testing him, almost constantly. It is as though she were trying to prove (to herself or to him, it is not clear) that he will turn out just like "all the other men in my life." The man is in a no-win situation and her ongoing tests and challenges are harming the relationship.

The woman in this example needs to work on herself. She needs to overcome the abuse she suffered and also the damage it caused her. She needs to understand what happened to her on the inside and how it happened. Only when she begins to trust herself again will she be able to trust someone else.

Healing Time

There are exceptions to everything, especially when dealing with human beings, but nearly all people who have been in controlling relationships and gotten out of them need some time, most probably alone, to heal and regain a good sense of perspective. When it comes to reconnecting and avoiding control, it takes more than being a free spirit, it takes knowing how to defend that freedom. It takes regaining a feeling of personal adequacy. It takes regaining the simple, childlike belief in yourself and your innate okayness. It takes getting back to a basic belief in yourself.

Healing from a controlling relationship means getting rid of the defenses and defensive attitude you may have had to develop to survive. You now have to regain some innocence. Just because your husband was a jerk does not mean that all men are jerks. Just because your wife manipulated you does not mean that all women are manipulative. You need to regain a balanced perspective.

Regaining lost innocence is not the same as becoming naive again. You should learn from your past experiences; the point is to not allow the past to blind you to the present. Yes, you have to be wary of problem traits in others that attract you, and of things inside you that blind you. But you also have to be fair to the next person who comes along. You cannot prejudge the person in your present based on people in your past, or you will become very cynical, and very lonely.

Yes, there will be more risks in the future. That can be very scary, but the fact is, relationships cannot develop without people taking risks. There is a natural tendency to overreact when you have been hurt. Mark Twain said that a cat who sits on a hot stove will never sit on another hot stove—but it will also never sit on a cold stove. You don't want to become that cat. You may have been burned, but you must regain your faith in people or you will not be able to let another person have a fair chance with you.

Some people can think their way through to that place of personal serenity and some need outside help. Again, much of it depends on what you have had to endure. Whatever it takes, you will need to invest time and energy in this healing process if you want to enter into another relationship with confidence.

Freedom and Commitment

When you are once again comfortable with yourself, with who you are and with who you are not, things will get easier. Once you have a clear perception of what you want in a partner and recognize that you are valuable enough to hold out until just the right person comes along, you feel better about relationships in general. Once you are ready to start looking, you will be looking for a relationship that can be both committed and free of controls.

What you want in a relationship is a safe harbor for your spirit—a place to call home. If you are insightful and fully in charge of your life, you know enough to choose the right place. In a sense, you are enlisting in a service. In return for dedicating your time and energy to the relationship, you obtain spiritual grounding. Everyone is grounded in something, whether or not they choose it. The need for spiritual grounding is universal.

Being free does not necessarily mean being free to do what you want all the time. But when you choose to make a commitment, you do so freely. You know that you are giving up a certain amount of freedom in exchange for something else. When people enlist in the military service, for example, they give up a certain amount of freedom. Enlistment means that you are no longer free for the next four years. The military is clear about that. In fact, military people no longer own themselves; they literally belong to the government.

But when people enlist in the military, it also means that they are acting voluntarily. They believe that they have a duty to their country. Many do not like the price in individuality that has to be paid to achieve the level of obedience that the military requires. But the point is that they are there by choice. They are still free on the inside.

When you make a commitment to another person, you are not grounded in the other person, just as the military person is not grounded in the government. It is concepts—not people or institutions—that ground you. Unfortunately, when it comes to relationships, too often people ground themselves in the concept of control.

Regrounding Yourself

Generally, this book has focused on learning how to un-ground yourself from the concept of control. Freeing yourself was a long and complicated process, but it was primarily a process of the mind. To be free, it is necessary to reject the concept of control as a way of life. Once that is done, then you can be free. You still need to be grounded, but you can be grounded in a relationship that will serve as a home base and also allow you to remain free.

Committing to a long-term relationship is, of course, quite different from joining the army. For one thing, there is no specific enlistment period, and, of course, the terms of the relationship are quite different: You are hopefully on an equal footing with your partner. Military service is also a relatively passive activity. You contract with the government to fulfill a very specific set of obligations.

There is nothing passive about human relationships. Your choice to remain in a relationship is ongoing and active. You may object and say that a marriage is also a contract, supposedly for life, but this is not really the case. Two people do not freeze in place—and the relationship does not freeze in place—at the time of the wedding. As you live and grow, you change and the relationship changes with you. So, the nature of this kind of contract, a committed relationship, has to be constantly reaffirmed as long as two people are together. That is why marriage is hard work and not to be taken for granted.

Remember also that control is a gradual process, that it does not happen in one day, or one week, or even one year. Often, it happens so slowly that the controlled person does not know what is happening until long after the control trap has been sprung. But even if you are not talking specifically about control, relationships change and evolve. There are other things that are unacceptable besides control that can make a person choose not to reaffirm the commitment. In order to be yourself, in order to live the way you choose to live, in order to remain free, you must retain the option to end a relationship when it becomes unacceptable.

How to Achieve Freedom Through Love and Commitment

When two people truly work on their relationship, it should grow stronger and closer and more loving with time. That is the whole point of being in a long-term relationship, to evolve together and to develop something that only gets better with the passage of time. So, if you want to ground yourself in something that allows you to be free, in what can you safely ground your spirit? There is only one thing that truly works and that is a love relationship. To truly understand this, you need to review the nature of a relationship free from control.

Remember, there are three prerequisites for love. The first of those is having total trust in your partner, knowing that it is safe to be fully vulnerable to your partner and knowing that your partner will never intentionally hurt you. The second is respecting your partner and being respected in return. It is only too true that respect seems to be the first thing to vanish when a relationship starts to deteriorate. The third prerequisite for love is friendship; friends look out for each other, love to be with each other, and can share things with each other.

With these prerequisites, there is really little or no room for control. Mutual freedom is a strong basis for trust because each of you knows that your partner's choice to be trustworthy is freely made and not based on control or obligation or any other lesser reason. It is a free decision and, therefore, a truly valuable decision. Mutual freedom is also the basis for respect. It is very difficult to respect someone who chooses to not be free. A controller does not really respect the person who is controlled. Power over another is a corrupting force. A person who is controlled does not respect his or her controller either. If anything, the feeling gradually evolves into loathing because there is a basic evil in the act of controlling. Finally, if your partner is your best friend, you want only the best for your partner. The very nature of friendship demands that each person freely choose to be friends. If that is not the case, it cannot really be called friendship.

Unconditional Love

A committed relationship must be based on unconditional love, loving a person exactly as he or she is. That kind of love has to include the mind, the body, and the spirit. But to love another person in this way is to work very hard to guard his or her freedom. To try to control is to try to make someone into somebody else. Even if you do not try to change any specific trait, the act of controlling causes a change. Love, real and unconditional love, includes a commitment to the freedom of the other person. It has to be that way because anything less takes you down the control path and control is a killer of real love. When you have a controlling relationship, you do not have real love. No matter how much someone may claim to be trying to hold onto someone else out of love, it is not love. It is insecurity. Real love and control cannot fit together.

Unconditional love also means allowing someone to evolve. You want what is best for the person you love, which is to say you want this person to advance and grow as much as possible. But you know it is not your job to figure out how someone needs to change. What you hope is that, as you each evolve into different people, your love will evolve too.

Respectful Communication

Another element in a healthy relationship is respectful communication. You need respectful communication to maintain the dignity of the relationship. Disrespect is intolerable. However, there is another way to look at this. If your partner is free, your partner will not tolerate disrespect, and if you are free, you will not tolerate disrespect. Freedom carries a certain amount of uncertainty, which makes people more careful in how they treat each other. You cannot afford to take each other for granted if you are free.

Accepting Differences

Accepting your differences really goes to the heart of freedom in a committed relationship. If you think about it, the things that make people different are internal. You have the choice of either accepting each other's uniqueness or rejecting it. If you choose to reject it, you are no longer grounded in love.

Learning from Each Other

You learn from each other through your differences. You can make your differences the targets for your own growth. In working with couples, the complementary nature of so many partners becomes increasingly clear. Often, each person in a relationship needs to move closer to the other, in order for each to improve. For example, if a very organized person forms a relationship with a very laid-back and spontaneous partner, one needs to relax and get more enjoyment out of life and the other needs to become more responsible. Couples in all types of relationships have things to teach one another. This idea of learning from one another creates the ultimate opportunity to form a cooperative relationship.

Cooperation vs. Competition

When two people want to be free, competition does not make sense. Yet our culture seems to be based on competition as the normal state of committed relationships. If forming and maintaining a cooperative relationship makes so much sense, why are people not doing it on a routine basis? To use the above example, an organized person criticizes a partner's spontaneity; the laid-back person thinks the other is incapable of having fun. Rather than learning from each other and moving toward each other, people try to force others to become more like them. You simply do not have time to waste on competition. When you compete, the spirit goes out of your relationship.

Joy: Each Other's Joy

If you truly love, it is the most natural thing in the world to share the happiness of your partner. Take, for example, the custom of giving presents. You do it for birthdays, Christmas, and on many other occasions. Sometimes you don't even need an occasion to give a present. You give presents because it feels good to see happiness in another.

Yet how can such feelings exist if you are not free? If there are strings attached to joy, it is no longer real joy. If you give a gift out of a sense of duty, or if you feel you have to pretend to like a gift, you are not feeling joy at the moment of giving and receiving. Joy can only truly be experienced in an atmosphere of freedom.

Accepting Your Partner's Freedom

It takes a great deal of courage to truly accept your partner as a free spirit. That is because the risk of losing your partner is enormous. But you must face and accept reality—and reality is that both you and your partner choose each other every single day. That choosing may be an active and conscious process or it can be a passive and unthinking process, but it does occur. This is why the feeling of inadequacy is so central to the process of control. It is when you feel you do not deserve what you have that you make safeguards to keep it. It is possible to become a controller even if you have been the controlled partner in previous relationships.

Remember, the more you accept your partner's freedom, the more likely it will be that your partner will continue to choose to be with you. If you want to be free, and you have a partner who also wants to be free, you have something really basic in common. To accept your partner's freedom and never do anything to knowingly challenge it is the greatest compliment, and the greatest validation of love, you can make. At the same time, you cannot have a healthy relationship without this acceptance.

Intimacy

It should come as no surprise that true intimacy needs freedom to exist and flourish. When you are free, you act out of that freedom, and your meaning cannot be misunderstood. To be loved by someone who is freely choosing to love you is the greatest form love can take.

Intimacy is a spiritual activity that most often is expressed physically. From the receiver's perspective, you know when you are freely being given intimacy and when you are manipulating the other person in order to receive it. There is an artificiality in coerced intimacy that cannot be mistaken.

Evolving Together

You have to be free to evolve, and if you want to evolve together, you have to give your partner room to evolve. In this way, you don't try to control each other.

If you decided what was best for your partner and tried to lead him or her along that path, you would not be helping. Actually, such an act would be more like manipulation. Sometimes you may think that what another person really needs is totally obvious. This is a common but very basic error to make. Even as you learn a major lesson in humility, you will gain great wisdom when you stop believing that you know what is good for somebody else.

What you can do with assurance is to encourage your partner, to cheer him or her on and to love unconditionally. You have to place your focus on your own evolution; that is where your efforts must be directed. Moving yourself forward is challenge enough. If you are lucky, you may find you have a partner who is encouraging you, cheering you on, loving you unconditionally, and not trying to channel your evolution into his or her idea of where it should go.

Parenting As a Team

The first chapter of this book covered how a young child is molded through interacting with his or her parents. You later looked at how your own parents and other factors in your life influenced you and had negative impacts on your self-esteem.

If you are a parent, you now have a great responsibility, but also a wonderful opportunity, to help your children maintain good self-esteem and learn to value themselves for who they are. Together, with your partner, you need to function as a parenting team to be the best parents for your child.

Granted, parenting is not the only thing that influences the development of children. But, through your parenting, you do have an opportunity to try to arm your children against the pitfalls they will encounter outside of your influence and later on in life. The importance of this opportunity cannot be over-emphasized. There is nothing more sacred than having a child and having the chance to help that child get started on his or her own journey.

To be most effective, you and your partner must share the same purpose. You need to agree on your parenting strategies. Together you can nurture confidence within your children. You can love them unconditionally, even while you discipline and teach the values you want them to have. You can teach them how to accept imperfections in themselves and to not demand the impossible. You can teach them how to prevent the insults of others from getting through the boundary of self-assurance. You can do so much.

By encouraging your child to accept imperfection, you are in no way suggesting that they stop competing or stop trying to better themselves. Just the opposite. Everyone has a duty to strive to reach his or her highest potential. People have the right to try their best to excel, and to wholeheartedly compete with others in whatever they choose as a challenge. But there is a great difference between trying to better yourself and trying to be what you are not.

You can give your children a boost in their attempt to fulfill their journey. You can surely help them to get past yourself. What can be better than to know your children are going to move ahead of you? If you could do nothing more than save them some of the struggles you had to endure to get to where you are, it would be an accomplishment. Where they go from the beginning point you give them is really up to them. But you at least have the opportunity to try to make things easier for them to get to their destination.

And now this work has truly come full circle. It has gone from exploring the development of feelings of inadequacy to the process of entering controlling relationships to the struggle it takes to get out of them again to the process of developing control-free relationships to the process of maintaining your freedom while in a committed relationship to, finally, the end: how to pass on the idea of lifelong freedom to the next generation. Many people spend years struggling to regain their freedom. Think of what tomorrow's adults could accomplish if they were shown ways to bypass that struggle. Think of the inner joy you would feel if you had the chance to see your children avoid all the pain and heartache you had to endure.

It doesn't get better than that.

Afterword

Well, it was a long journey we have just taken together. At the beginning, I had two goals for you to take from this. The first was for you to truly know that you are not alone, that there are many people struggling to find themselves under the weight of a basic lack of faith in themselves and the ever deepening feelings of personal loss that is so much a part of control. The other thing I hoped you would see is that the formation of a controlling relationship is a process, something that happens between two people. I wanted you to understand that, as a process, it can be changed, even reversed. You may feel totally under the power and domination of another person, but the truth is that the control only works if you continue to participate in the process.

There are a lot of people who have talked with me about their situations. Many of them were convinced they were helpless, with no options. Some had very good rationalizations that helped them maintain their belief in their helplessness. Some even surrendered those beliefs. It is true that every circumstance is different. Some people are in worse positions than others. Many have given in to financial tyranny and feel they cannot make any changes because they would never be able to afford to live on their own. Others have convinced themselves that they are helpless because their children are involved. People have developed many reasons for feeling trapped by controllers. But the bottom line of control is nevertheless that it will only work if both people, the controller as well as the controlled, participate in the relationship. This is a hard thing to believe, especially if the control pattern is deeply entrenched in the relationship, but it is true, nonetheless.

If you are in a controlling relationship and truly want to be free it can be done. If you want to be the person you were when you started this journey of life, it can happen. However, you must be willing to fight for yourself. To do that, you must believe that you are worth fighting for, that you are worth the struggle. There is also a price that you must be willing to pay. I cannot predict what that price will be. Maybe there is a formula that can be worked out some day that will match the level of entrenchment in control and the price you can expect to pay to get out of it. But at this point, all I can say is it varies from situation to situation.

The truth is, if overcoming a controlling relationship were free and painless, you would not have read this book. Ultimately, it boils down to a simple faith—if you truly believe that you are worthy of personal freedom, and worthy of a relationship that is healthy and not based on control, then you also have to believe that the answers, that the means, will come to you.

Richard J. Stenack, Ph.D., is a psychologist in private practice specializing in issues of control. He lives in Norwalk, Ohio.

Photo by Tammy Roberts

Some Other
New Harbinger Titles

The Anxiety & Phobia Workbook, 3rd edition, Item PHO3 $19.95

Beyond Anxiety & Phobia, Item BYAP $19.95

The Self-Nourishment Companion, Item SNC $10.95

The Healing Sorrow Workbook, Item HSW $17.95

The Daily Relaxer, Item DALY $12.95

Stop Controlling Me!, Item SCM $13.95

Lift Your Mood Now, Item LYMN $12.95

An End to Panic, 2nd edition, Item END2 $19.95

Serenity to Go, Item STG $12.95

The Depression Workbook, Item DEP $19.95

The OCD Workbook, Item OCD $18.95

The Anger Control Workbook, Item ACWB $17.95

Flying without Fear, Item FLY $14.95

The Shyness & Social Anxiety Workbook, Item SHYW $15.95

The Relaxation & Stress Reduction Workbook, 5th edition, Item RS5 $19.95

Energy Tapping, Item ETAP $14.95

Stop Walking on Eggshells, Item WOE $14.95

Angry All the Time, Item ALL 12.95

Living without Procrastination, Item $12.95

Hypnosis for Change, 3rd edition, Item HYP3 $16.95

Don't Take it Personally, Item DOTA $15.95

Toxic Coworkers, Item TOXC $13.95

Letting Go of Anger, Item LET $13.95

Call **toll free, 1-800-748-6273,** or log on to our online bookstore at **www.newharbinger.com** to order. Have your Visa or Mastercard number ready. Or send a check for the titles you want to New Harbinger Publications, Inc., 5674 Shattuck Ave., Oakland, CA 94609. Include $4.50 for the first book and 75¢ for each additional book, to cover shipping and handling. (California residents please include appropriate sales tax.) Allow two to five weeks for delivery.

Prices subject to change without notice.